GHAM

WN

AR

SAVING FAITH

SAVING FAITH

We are unto God
a sweet savour of Christ,
in them that are saved
II Cor. 2:15

JOHN METCALFE

THE PUBLISHING TRUST
Church Road, Tylers Green, Penn, Buckinghamshire.

Printed and Published by
John Metcalfe Publishing Trust
Church Road, Tylers Green,
Penn, Buckinghamshire

—

First Published January 1992

—

ISBN 1 870039 40 8

—

6003608717

CONTENTS

THE ALARM

I

The Alarm

THAT work of salvation by which a sinner is brought to saving faith begins in the soul with the sounding of God's alarm. As with every work of God in salvation this is wrought within by the power of the Holy Ghost, acting in concert with the word of God. Consider therefore this initial work of God in the saving of the soul:

1. THE SOUNDING OF THE ALARM

An alarm is a loud noise, cry, or amplified sound designed to AWAKEN SWIFTLY, either from sleep, or to a danger of which one is otherwise unaware, or both.

In the old testament the alarm was sounded by the BLOWING OF THE TRUMPET. The spiritual and new testament meaning of this old testament figure refers to the breath or wind of the Holy Ghost blasting the reality of the word of God into the soul, so that it sounds in a way never before realised.

This trumpet sound awakens sinners and backsliders to that danger—that very real danger—to which otherwise they are as insensible as a man in a dead sleep. The initiative is taken by God, by the Holy Ghost, to those slumbering on in oblivion, as good as dead men: these are awakened by sounding an alarm upon the trump of God. And this was the old-fashioned method of preaching which has virtually disappeared in our

1

own day. Nevertheless, it is the first step in the work of the Spirit to awaken and bring the sinner to saving faith in Christ.

This interior sound of the Spirit's trumpet is the commencement of the work, because without it, the sinner is dead asleep and utterly unconscious of danger. But, Ezek. 33:3, He shall blow the trumpet, and warn the people. Numb. 10:9, Ye shall blow an alarm with the trumpets. Zeph. 1:16, Behold, a day of the trumpet and alarm. Jer. 4:19, The sound of the trumpet, the alarm. II Chron. 13:12, With sounding trumpets to cry alarm. In which the breath or wind blown through the instrument makes an alarming noise, waking up those otherwise insensitive to their danger. Just so the breath of the Spirit blows through the instrument of the word of God to the piercing of the sleep of death in the carnal soul that is at ease, unconscious in slumber despite the desperate dangers lying just the other side death.

This sound ruptures the membrane of the inner ear of the soul, giving an ear-splitting, soul-shattering blast that rends the natural uncircumcision of the heart and ears to warn of things hitherto unheard, unfelt, and unknown. Suddenly the trumpet blast alerts the soul to a staggering awareness of the reality of God. The seriousness of death. The existence of the law. The fact of sin. The guiltiness of the soul. The certainty of the judgment to come. The verity of the resurrection of the dead. The dreadfulness of the wrath to come. The awfulness of a fixed eternity. The brevity of time. The vanity of a passing world. Under this alarming blast, all these truths, in the felt consciousness of them, now powerfully penetrate the most inward parts of the soul.

Now the trumpet is blown on the tenth day of the soul, now the LORD is gone up with the sound of a trumpet, now, Jer. 49:2, God causeth an alarm of war to be heard! Now is felt the sound of an alarm, now the seven angels begin to sound in the inward parts of the soul, now the impending wrath is felt, and, trembling, the soul prepares to forsake all and flee from the wrath to come.

The sinner, having the inward ears opened where before they were shut fast and sealed, cries to his own soul: Sanctify a fast: sound an alarm: cry unto the LORD! In the midnight of the soul a great cry is heard: THE BRIDEGROOM COMETH: PREPARE TO MEET HIM! Mt. 25:6, At midnight there was a cry made, Behold, the bridegroom cometh. Now, Isa. 42:14, The soul cries like a travailing woman, for there is, Heb. 12:19, The sound of a trumpet, and the voice of words, and, Rev. 4, A voice like a trumpet crying. It is, Mt. 3:3, The voice of one crying in the wilderness of the soul, saying, Isa. 58:1, Cry aloud, and spare not, lift up thy voice like a trumpet, and show my people their transgression, and the house of Jacob their sins.

The blast thereof breaks the pitchers which had shielded the penetrating light of conscience, it brings down the walls of the soul at the sounding of the rams' horns, exposing it to the wrath and vengeance of Almighty God. For the trumpet soundeth long, Ex. 19:13, Thou hearest the sound thereof but canst not tell whence it cometh nor whither it goeth, Jn. 3:8, but of a truth, it gives no uncertain sound, I Cor. 14:8.

The sinner is now fully awakened to the wrath of God. This is revealed from heaven, not generally, but against oneself, and revealed within the soul. The native enmity against God now comes to light, terror, fearfulness and trembling take hold on one, the sorrows of death compass the soul, the sorrows of hell compass it about, the snares of death are set all around, and the poor sinner cries out in alarm, warned to sue for peace from a God set upon wrath, to cry for mercy from a God who cannot be found, from whom nothing but wrath and indignation can be felt, and, desperate, THE SOUL HAS BECOME THOROUGHLY ALARMED. This is the first part of the work. Now follows the second.

But I pause to ask, How many today have come even so far as the first? For today is the day in which they climb into the sheepfold some other way: but to their everlasting shame. And who, today, even preaches this, the plain old-fashioned gospel truth, by which sinners of old invariably came to experience salvation? If you say, But we never heard such preachers in our lives, I reply, Well, you are hearing one now, and make a new, a good foundation while you may, as did Christian in Bunyan's 'Pilgrim's Progress', which, if you read, describes precisely this process, when Evangelist wakes up the slumbering sinner at carnal ease in the city doomed to destruction, with the dreadful cry 'Flee from the wrath to come!' This is the alarm; the next work of God follows.

THE AWAKENING

II

The Awakening

2. The Awakening

'AWAKE thou that sleepest, and arise from the dead, and Christ shall give thee light' comes the cry. But this light is no soft rosy glow, for its beams are terrible to the soul, reproving one's sins, lighting up the inward recesses to reveal a cave of uncleanness and depravity, unbelief and enmity, and at bottom a black fountain welling up with filth and corruption. The same light reveals God terrible in majesty, awful in his holiness, unbending in his righteousness, the very sky seeming to flame with the fiery portent of the wrath to come. This awakes the soul from its dreams: It is, Awake to judgment; Awake, awake, stand up, O Jerusalem! I Cor. 15:34, Awake to righteousness, and sin not. Rom. 13:11, It is high time to awake out of sleep.

Before the alarm sounded, all was dark, nothing was heard, nothing was felt. The reality was the dream, and the dream was the reality: NOW IT IS ALL SHATTERED. Now the deadening slumber of the world which held one fast as in an all enveloping cocoon is utterly cast off, and the soul sees with horror that the whole world has been deceived! That the whole profession of Christianity is in a dead sleep! Alarmed by the blast of God's trumpet within the soul; awakened to the reality of one's dreadful state before a God out of Christ; THE WHOLE WORLD IS SEEN AS LYING IN DARKNESS, IN THE POWER OF THE WICKED ONE. What an awakening this proves to be!

7

The silver trumpets have sounded; the rams' horns have blasted; the walls have come down; the light has broken in. Now God cries to the heart, AWAKE, AWAKE! The Spirit paints the day of judgment upon the canvas of the soul: then, Oh, then what distance from a holy, an inaccessible God of righteousness, what sin, what guilt, what hardness, what unbelief, what helplessness: NOW THE LAW APPEARS IN ITS TERRIBLE, INEXORABLE, IMMUTABLE MAJESTY. NOW THE CURSE SOUNDS. NOW SIN REVIVES, AND THE SOUL DIES, CRYING, The law is holy, and just, and good; but I am carnal, sold under sin.

Bankruptcy and ruin face the insolvent debtor, with eternity to languish in hell over debts never paid in time. Desperate, the soul casts about for mercy, but the law knows no mercy. It seeks for some commandments to keep, but, awakened to the spirituality of the law, it finds that it breaks them all in heart. Hopeless, despairing, the awakened sinner cries: Thine arrows stick fast in me, and thy hand presseth me sore: mine iniquities are gone over mine head. I am troubled. I am bowed down greatly. I go mourning all the day long.

At last the soul begins to pray, for the first time in its life. Now this becomes the language of the heart: 'Deliver me from all my transgressions: make me not the reproach of the foolish; Remove thy stroke away from me: I am consumed by the blow of thine hand.' Oh, says the soul, 'I was dumb; I opened not my mouth; because THOU didst it.'

Oh, how profound the awakening, how deep the convictions, when GOD does it! The natural man knows nothing of this. These spiritual things are foolishness to him. The vast, vast mass of Christianity, so called, never had these experiences. They went to their priests, their pastors, their ministers, their evangelists, their Brethren elders, their gospel hall leaders, and were told 'Just accept Jesus'. 'Never mind your feelings, trust the word only.' 'Let Jesus into your heart.' AND THUS THESE BLIND GUIDES LEAD THE BLIND, UTTERLY OVERTURNING EVERY

OLD LANDMARK, QUITE OBLITERATING THE FOOTSTEPS OF THE FLOCK, AND BLOTTING OUT THE WAYS AND PATHS OF THE LORD.

But 'To the law and to the testimony; if they speak not according to this word, it is because there is no light in them.' No, all their light is artificial, and glows on nothing but the dead, outward letter, in which they say they trust. Just as all their works are done for to be seen of men. Now, when all this has taken place, there follows the work of God called Conviction.

CONVICTION

III

Conviction

3. CONVICTION

THIS has nothing to do with man, or with legal preaching, or with the dead letter of scripture, or with the natural conscience: this is of God. It is a divine work. It comes from heaven. 'Now a thing was secretly brought to me, and mine ear received a little thereof. In thoughts from the visions of the night, when deep sleep falleth on men, fear came upon me, and trembling, which made all my bones to shake. Then a spirit passed before my face; the hair of my flesh stood up: it stood still, but I could not discern the form thereof'—No; thou knowest not whence it cometh, nor whither it goeth— 'and I heard a voice, saying, SHALL MORTAL MAN BE MORE JUST THAN GOD?'

The effect of such a question, divinely uttered in the terror of the LORD from heaven, penetrating the inmost conscience and heart by revelation, I say, the effect of such a question is to make a man say, and say with his belly and mouth cleaving to the dust of the earth, 'I have heard of thee with the hearing of the ear, but now mine eye seeth thee, and I abhor myself in dust and ashes.' 'Depart from me, O Lord, for I am a sinful man.' 'Woe is me! for I am undone, because I am a man of unclean lips, and I dwell in the midst of a people of unclean lips.' 'There remaineth no strength in me: for my comeliness is turned in me to corruption, and I retain no strength.' 'Behold, I am vile.'

13

Now all self-righteousness and legal striving is laid in the dust, and the soul language is: 'God be merciful to me, a sinner.' This is preceded by the alarm, by the awakening, and is called Conviction. This is accompanied by a beating of the breast, a casting down of the eyes to the earth. Here is the man who prays, not he who barely repeats words under the guidance of false prophets, fools and blind! And yet even the man who so prays, who is so convicted, is still very far from saving faith. But he is in the way. He is convicted, and that of Almighty God from heaven, and by nothing less than divine rays of revelation to the inward heart and conscience, making the sinner bitterly, feelingly aware of the majesty of God, his absolute holiness, as against man's foul depravity.

Now the soul is pricked to the heart, and cries 'What must I do to be saved?' Now he is 'convicted of his own conscience.' Now, such are 'convinced of the law as transgressors.' This makes the humble soul to turn at God's reproof. And 'he that heareth reproof getteth understanding': thus the soul gains the beginning of wisdom, and fears the LORD. It trembles at his word from a broken and contrite heart, it is made to tremble and be astonished at God's reproof.

Yet the convicted soul would not escape from these heart-breaking experiences to gain the whole world: it knows that this is the only way to be brought to saving faith, it knows this cutting reproof, this convicting goad, is profitable for doctrine, for reproof, for correction in righteousness. The grateful language of the soul is this: 'Let the righteous smite me; it shall not break mine head.' Since it is God that said, Psalm 50, 'I will reprove thee', the answer of the broken-hearted, contrite and meek soul follows, 'Thou hast convicted me'. The soul says, 'Against thee, thee only have I sinned, and done this evil in thy sight, that thou mightest be justified when thou speakest, and clear when thou judgest.'

The soul comes to the light by that same Holy Ghost from whom the light came to the soul: in coming to this light, its deeds are reproved, its sins rebuked of God. In the light of God's countenance all the soul's secret sins are made bare; then, great fear comes upon the soul, it begins to work out its own salvation with fear and trembling, pressing forward to settled, saving faith with a witness. The soul knows who it is that is working within its heart, though not yet brought to him; yet with the smallest light of a candle shining—though often obscured—in the inner man, there is a secret conviction that THIS WORK IS OF GOD, and that what God begins he will surely complete.

Great fear comes upon all who are brought under this convicting work, even unto trembling. This demonstrates how spurious is the kind of thing that passes for faith today, for the prayer of such a convicted soul, though still far, far short of saving faith, is put by Christendom into the mouth of every vain fool, every trivial joker, every light trifler, and, having said 'The sinner's prayer', as they call it, such empty, chaffy creatures are told not to rely on feelings, no, they are surely saved, they are brought to faith! So are devils, to such a faith! With this difference: the devils believe, AND TREMBLE.

But as to those who are to be brought to the faith of God's elect, even to like precious faith with the saints and the apostles, all these come another way, by a different path. Far short of saving faith, though certain of it in the end, having been alarmed, having been awakened, in a state, a feeling state, of conviction of sin from the interior work of the Holy Ghost, these share the experiences common to God's people from the beginning.

Thus we read in Exodus: Fear and dread fell upon them; his fear was before their face: they served the LORD in fear, waiting upon him, Psalm 2; they chose the fear of the LORD, Prov. 1. Knowing that the fear of the LORD is to hate evil, and the fear of the LORD is the beginning of wisdom, therefore they perfected holiness in the fear of God, so far as they had gone in their real experience. For the fear of the LORD prolongeth days, and hence they sought him with singleness of heart in the fear of God, for God saith, The fear of the LORD is a fountain of life, declaring, Fear the LORD, ye his saints. Hence the convicted soul responds, My flesh trembleth for fear of thee, Psalm 119, observing that God's covenant with Levi was of life and peace for the fear wherewith he feared before God, and that they that feared the LORD and thought upon his name were had in remembrance before God. Whence it follows that the convicted soul is grateful from the heart, trembling at God's rebuke.

And, indeed, 'Open rebuke is better than secret love.' Hence the convicted soul, Heb. 12:5, does not faint when he is rebuked of God, for, Rev. 3:19, as many as Christ loves—and none other—he rebukes and chastens. Indeed, several times over in the gospels it is said, Jesus rebuked his disciples.

And he does so still, by his faithful ministers, saying, Rebuke them sharply, Titus 1:13, and, Rebuke them with all authority, Titus 2:15, besides, Them that sin rebuke before all, I Tim. 5:20. Christ admonishes his ministers, II Tim. 4:2, Rebuke with all longsuffering and doctrine.

At this the convicted soul, cut to the heart, is brought very low and humble, being unable honestly to come up so high as these cutting reproofs require, convinced thereby of being short of saving faith. But this causes the soul to seek the harder, the more earnestly, and with a more single eye, God crushing the natural and imperious pride with his soul-shattering word, saying, Jer. 5:22, Fear ye not me? saith the LORD: will ye not tremble at my presence?

For one day, when it is too late, All people shall tremble and fear before him, and the mountains shall see him and tremble. But not to salvation; and this makes the convicted soul to shake for fear. Thus convicted souls, brought by

16

God's law to humble themselves, brought to the fear of God, answer to what is written, Ex. 19:16, The people that was in the camp trembled. So saith Job: At this also my heart trembled. And Ezra commanded in the word of the LORD, Every one that trembleth at the word of God. And it must be so, Psalm 99, The LORD reigneth; let the people tremble.

As Paul reasoned, Felix trembled, Acts 24:25, for that was the invariable effect of preaching the gospel—fully, and from the beginning—with the Holy Ghost sent down from heaven. Nowadays, however, they neither preach the gospel, much less fully, nor does so much as even their corrupt version of the bible comprehend it, and far, far from being with the Holy Ghost sent down from heaven, today it is all in the flesh, and to accommodate the worldly. But Job testifies of the way of God from the beginning, 'A trembling took hold of my flesh', and Paul witnesses how the early saints received the ministry, II Cor. 7:15, 'With fear and trembling'.

What a work, then, when GOD convicts! Where are these convictions today? Tell me, where? Where in modern evangelism? Enquire, how many in the so-called 'churches' have received them, or even look for them? Say, how many so-called 'ministers' preach them, or even admit of their existence? For of what use are the so-called fundamentalists, or traditional Protestants, as they think of themselves, when it comes to these things? What have the wretched, deluded sect of the charismatics to do with this? They have all like sheep gone astray: they have turned every one to his own way. 'There is none that understandeth: there is none that seeketh after God. They are all gone out of the way, they are together become unprofitable; there is none that doeth good, no, not one. There is no fear of God before their eyes.'

Hence it has happened to the Gentiles as Paul warned of the Jews. At the end of their times they, the Jews, the natural branches of Israel, were broken off the stock of God's olive

17

tree, and we, the Gentile nations, at the beginning of our time, were, though wild branches, grafted in to that stock.

Two thousand years have passed, during which the whole Jewish nation has been cut off in unbelief. Of this, Paul warned us to beware. But we have not taken heed. We cared not, nor did our fathers care, how to come to saving faith, neither did we choose, nor our fathers, how to come to saving faith by the infallible marks and steps that lead to it in the work of God. No, we chose false faith, dead-letter belief, easy believism, persuasion over texts, prating like fools, 'But it is not a matter of feelings'. That is, we chose unbelief, and spurned the way of faith. AND NOW WE ARE BROKEN OFF, AS SURELY AND AS CERTAINLY AS WERE THE JEWS IN THEIR DAY TWO THOUSAND YEARS AGO. So God has broken off and departed from the Gentile churches. And wherefore? 'Because of unbelief.'

Thus, as the prophet cried unto Israel, so we testify to the Gentile 'Christians': 'Though the number of the children of Israel be as the sand of the sea'—yea, even as the profession of Christ, and the whole of Christianity—only 'a remnant shall be saved.' As he saith before, 'Except the Lord of Sabaoth had left us a seed,. we had been as Sodoma, and been made like unto Gomorrha.'

'Even so at this time there is a remnant according to the election of grace', as there was at that time two thousand years ago. But where are they? Outside the camp of Christendom, as that remnant was outside the camp of Judaism. 'Let us go forth therefore unto him without the camp, bearing his reproach', Heb. 13:13. But how shall we know the way? It is as it ever was, through the straight gate of a sound conversion, and along the narrow way of saving faith. But how shall we find the gate? It is being described to you. First, you knew not so much as whether there be any gate. But the ALARM sounded; then the cry, AWAKE to righteousness; next, came the arrows

18

of God's CONVICTION, as his hand pressed you sore. 'This is the way: walk ye in it.' There is no other pathway to saving faith in the gospel of Christ.

This, The alarm; The awakening; conviction of sin, is that work of God prior to quickening by which God brings his own elect to saving faith. 'Ah', say some, 'Not so: there is no need of such a prior work of the Spirit: only believe! Venture only! Ignore your frames and feelings; simply accept Jesus from the bible.' So said Spurgeon; so said J.N. Darby: easy believers both, and lovers of the same. Not so the prophets. Not so the apostles. 'For if I should yet please men, I should not be the servant of Christ.' Hearken to the men of God, despised by the world, hated by the already falling churches, loathed and envied by the so-called 'ministry': men such as Bunyan, Huntington, and others equally rejected and despised in their day, heaped with lies, slander, and libel. 'Of whom the world was not worthy.'

But what saith the scripture? Hearken to the Spirit's voice in the bible, that is, the bible of your fathers, through which he speaks. No prior work of the Spirit to bring sinners to Christ? The bible in itself teaches that just as the old testament preceded the new in the history of mankind, so it must precede the new in the history of the soul, that is, in the inward reception of it. First it must be 'Blessed is the man whom thou chastenest O LORD, and teachest out of thy law.' And is this blessing and teaching not a prior work before coming to Christ? So far from faith being without a prior work, there can be no coming to faith in Christ without such a preparation! Christ himself taught, 'No man can come to me, except the Father which hath sent me, draw him', Jn. 6:44. By definition, this drawing is a prior work.

Again, Jesus saith, 'They shall be all taught of God. Every man therefore that hath heard, and hath learned of the Father, cometh unto me', Jn. 6:45. Where the being taught of

God, the hearing, the learning from the Father, ALL PRECEDED THEIR COMING TO CHRIST. Taught of God? Taught what? Why, the law, for the old testament preceded the new, and this you must learn in your own soul, as it is written, Blessed is the man whom thou chastenest O LORD, and teachest out of thy law. And hearing what? Why, AN ALARM, as we have shown you. And learning what? Why TO AWAKEN, and press with all your heart, mind, understanding, and strength through the gate and on the way to SAVING FAITH, by the which you shall surely be brought to Christ.

Just as Adam came before Christ, Elijah before Elisha, Moses before Jesus, the law before the gospel, so these things must come to the heart of all those called of God out of the Fall, out of the city of destruction, before they can come in truth, and by the Spirit, to Christ, and to the city of God. There were two Jerusalems, Galatians 4, and not until the Jerusalem below is detested, and fled from by spiritual experience, will any come to Jerusalem above by the revelation from on high. Hence we say, 'If I forget thee, O Jerusalem, let my right hand forget her cunning. If I do not remember thee, let my tongue cleave to the roof of my mouth; if I prefer not Jerusalem above my chief joy', Psalm 137. Now, evidently, this is not Jerusalem below, because John calls that spiritual Sodom and Egypt, and Paul designates it the city which is in bondage with her children. Then the psalmist must be speaking of Jerusalem above, which he loved fervently, being the city of liberty, with her free-born sons. Whence this love? Because he had first tasted bondage, and the burden of the legal rule. This is the soul's experience: the one precedes the other.

Thus John the baptist preceded Jesus historically: and his ministry must precede Christ's spiritually. For it is within that the way of the LORD must first be prepared: by bringing down all the haughty hills, every mountain of pride; by exalting all the low places of heart despair, of sinking unbelief, all the valleys of soul desperation; by straightening all the crooked deceits, the twisted guile; by removing all the lusts, envies, jealousies that block the path. The ministry that does this is alarming, it is awakening, it is convicting: yes, but it surely leads to Christ.

Just so in the parable of the sower: the state of the ground preceded the coming of the sower. The ground was already wayside; or shallow; or filled with the seeds of thorns; or else perfectly good, BEFORE the sower came. When he came, he sowed ON THAT GROUND. He did not prepare it. What was to be prepared, had been prepared. He sowed. That is all. BUT THE PREPARATION WORK DETERMINED THE ISSUE. Only the prepared good ground received the seed to profit. The rest was lost. Now tell me there is no need for a preparation work, only 'believe' as such as Spurgeon and Darby presume, ignore your feelings, just come. Oh, no: not according to Jesus: ONLY BE PREPARED, and that of God.

The same holds good in Paul's exposition of the gospel. Romans 1:18 to 3:20 expounds the beginning of the gospel of our salvation. But they are chapters, alarming chapters, waking up the soul to sin, wrath, law, the commandment, the curse, the rebellion and enmity of man, bringing the soul that receives it prostrate in a living death, slain by the convicting power of God's word. THEN comes the knowledge of Christ in saving faith, Romans 3:21 to 5:21. First the word is as fire and a hammer that breaketh the rock in pieces. Then as oil and wine poured in to heal the wounded soul. First must come the poverty of spirit, then the kingdom of heaven; first the mourning, then the comfort; first the being made meek, then the inheritance; first the hungering and thirsting, then the righteousness of faith.

First the distress then the relief. First the preparation work then the work for which one is prepared. So saith the doctrine of Christ: 'Blessed be ye poor; blessed are ye that hunger now;

blessed are ye that weep now; blessed are ye when men shall hate you, and when they shall separate you from their company, and shall reproach you, and cast out your name as evil, for the Son of man's sake.' Now all these things are brought in by a prior work: the poverty by an alarm; the hunger by an awakening; the weeping from conviction; the being hated by the world, and worldly religion, from God's choosing us out of the world, and his drawing us to Christ by this preparation work, which the world and worldly religion rejects, but at the same time envies with bitter hatred because God has chosen us for this work, and not them. And all this is but to debase us by showing forth his mercy, that all the praise might be to the riches of his grace.

No prior work? First one must discover one's leprosy, then be cleansed. First the blindness, then the sight. First the lameness, then the leaping as an hart. First the deafness, then the hearing of the alarm. First the sleep of death, then the awakening. First the palsy, then the taking up of the bed to walk. First the dumbness, then the loosing of the tongue. First the sepulchre of the dead soul, then the resurrection and the life by the voice of the Son of God. Every convicted person knows these things, because every convicted person has experienced them. But it is not yet saving faith. Only, whoso has come this far, is as certain of glory as if he were already there. But whoso denies these things forsakes his own mercy, bringing down a curse upon his own soul, by shutting himself out from the salvation of God.

Now, all that has led up to this convicting work, including the work itself, from THE ALARM, through THE AWAKENING to the work of CONVICTION, has been wrought through the PENETRATION OF SOUND, and the INSHINING OF LIGHT from God upon and within the soul.

QUICKENING

IV

Quickening

W HAT follows after these beginnings leads to an entirely new divine communication. THE CRUCIAL COMMUN-ICATION. It is neither the communication of sound, as with the alarm; nor is it the communication of light, as in conviction: QUICKENING IS THROUGH THE COMMUNICATION OF LIFE.

But just as the sound was divine, it came from above; and just as the light was of God, it came from heaven: both coming through the word, yet, withal, both elevated above that word, coming from God himself in glory to the interior of the soul: EVEN MORE SO WITH THE LIFE. Divine life excels all that proceeds from him: it is *himself*, in person, a communication at once divine, supernatural, spiritual, mysterious, and heavenly. Following on from the sound and light of God from above breaking in, here appears a deeper, more immediate communication. Not now *from* his presence: this *is* his presence.

This communication of life is called QUICKENING, and is the distinct fourth operation, in sequence, of the work of God in bringing the soul to saving faith. But because it is not wrought by the sound of his voice only; nor the light from his presence simply; but, including both, it intensifies to the coming of himself in his own person, his divine nature, to the inward parts of the soul. It is a watershed: it is *the* crucial point.

4. QUICKENING

I. Consider, firstly, THE IMPLICATIONS OF QUICKENING

(i) What this implies as to nature

It implies death. This by definition. A sick man is not quickened. However near he may be to death's door, his life is still in him. It is not the quickening of life but the saving of his health that he needs. He is yet quick. He is yet alive. But in contrast to the live, or quick, there are the dead. It is the quick and the dead. It is the dead that need quickening, not the live, or those already quick. Then quickening implies that the nature, human nature, and the quality of its being which we thought of as life, GOD DENIES AS BEING LIFE. He calls it DEATH. Nature, human nature, human life, he regards as in a state of death. Hence, before anything at all can come before God as acceptable, there must first be a quickening.

But how quicken men that scoff at such a notion, being so confident of human nature, and so convinced of the living quality of their being? Even if never so feeble, if dreadfully sick, still, their own consciousness, supported by all mankind, denies that they are yet dead. Then quickening is not necessary in their eyes: much less in the eyes of the healthy.

Then how is it to become necessary, in the eyes of those whom God has determined to bring to saving faith? Only by his bringing them out of their delusions, to the truth; out of their blindness, to sight; out of their inward darkness, to the light of Christ.

But HOW? By sounding an alarm to these dead sleepers. By waking them up. By convicting them of the truth. Then though dead still, yet in the awareness of their human nature, in the consciousness of their human being, this mighty blast of the trumpet in the soul, this being shaken awake, this piercing of the arrows of conviction will all serve notice that their so-called 'life' is but a delusion. It will register in their consciousness 'this is not life: it is a living death!' This will give testimony in their awareness 'I am dead to God, dead to all spiritual life, I am incapable of knowing, seeing, or communicating with him.' That is, alarmed, awakened, convicted, the dead soul, as to human awareness, has by the sound of God's voice, and by the light from his presence, become aware of its dead condition. Then it cries for quickening. Because the soul knows that it is not merely sick: it is utterly dead. Not as to the body, towards man; but as to the soul, towards God. Nothing alerts men to this reality save God's prior alarm, awakening, and convicting work. And none, but none, will be quickened save those who know their dead state beforehand, confessing the same from the heart in consequence of the preparatory work of God.

Of this actual state of death to which natural living men are completely oblivious, scripture bears abundant testimony: Speaking of those who professed to be of Christ, yet had not the love of God in them, which love issued forth as a fountain of life in the living to all the brethren in Christ, John says 'He that loveth not his brother abideth in death', I Jn. 3:14. Abideth in it: he was never quickened out of a permanent—abiding—state of death, his profession of faith was nothing but lip-service, a vain outward show. Again, Rom. 7:24, the poor convicted man cries 'Who shall deliver me from the body of this death?' But his body was not dead, it was alive: how could it be a body of death? Because natural life, to the man that sought God, was a state of living death. Whoso feels it not, is neither alarmed, nor awakened, much less convicted: he is dead.

So saith Paul, Eph. 2:1, where he speaks of the saints having been dead in trespasses and sins. Thus it is with the whole of mankind born in Adam, the man of sin and death,

27

trespasses and sins frame the coffin around the dead life of the natural man, though the world knows it not. The entire world, in all its generations, the whole race, is blind to it. But the Ephesians, having been convicted, crying for life from the dead, had been brought to the truth. And, calling upon God, who heard their cry, it followed, 'And you hath he quickened, who WERE dead.' As was the whole unconvicted world; and as is a false and fallen profession of dead religion in the letter, even to this very day.

That the state of the unconverted world is a state of death, not of the body but the soul, appears in Col. 2:13, 'You, being dead in your sins'; which the Colossians were, till quickened. So that the state of nature, or carnality, remains a living death, so deceitful because the world is quite blind to this condition of deadness in which it is minded to live, for, Rom. 8:6, 'To be carnally minded is death'. And, Rom. 8:2, nothing but the Spirit of life, quickening within the soul, makes one 'free from the law of sin and death'. Beneath this law of death lies the whole deluded world, and the entire mass of worldly religion. Hence, Jn. 5:24, only those who, having been alarmed, awakened, convicted, in a word, having been taught of God, hear Jesus' word and 'pass from death unto life'. Otherwise the entire world and all its religion lies fast under bondage to this dead condition, hence, I Tim. 5:6, 'She that liveth in pleasure is dead while she liveth'.

The way, the only way, of understanding comes by the light from heaven shining into the soul, leading the alarmed, awakened, convicted sinner to the place where God quickens into life. But, Prov. 21:16, 'He that wandereth out of the way of understanding shall remain in the congregation of the dead.' That is, the state of nature, religious in the world and in the profession of the dead letter, with a Christ of bare outward texts, is called, 'the congregation of the dead'. Nevertheless, the Son of God quickens into life all those dead souls, now convicted of their state, drawn to him of the Father, saying,

'The hour is coming, AND NOW IS, when the dead shall hear the voice of the Son of God: and they that hear'—and none other—'shall live', Jn. 5:25. None other, for, Jn. 6:53, 'Except ye eat the flesh of the Son of man, and drink his blood, ye have no life in you.' Hence, I Jn. 5:12, 'He that hath not the Son of God hath not life.'

Thus the scriptures, the Lord Jesus, and the holy apostles join in one to testify and warn the world that it is deluded into supposing that what it has is life: the state of nature is not life: it is death. The worldly man, the natural man, is as dead towards God, as those in the graveyards are towards him. The so-called 'living' live in the sleep of death, hastening on to the resurrection and the judgment to come, oblivious to all. Like the dead in the graves, their state is that to which they are oblivious. In Adam not only all die bodily, but another kind of death passes from Adam to all men, and for the same reason, namely, because all have sinned in the Fall. This is the living death of nature. This interior death is total, it reigns over all the world. 'For God sent his only begotten Son into the world, that we might live through him', I Jn. 4:9. If so, the world must be dead without him. For, Jn. 6:33, 'The bread of God is he which cometh down from heaven, and giveth life unto the world.' Then, without that bread, the world is dead.

For the world has no life in itself. And, said Jesus, 'The bread that I will give is my flesh, which I will give for the life of the world', Jn. 6:51. But if the world had life, then his giving of his flesh for the life of the world would have been superfluous: its necessity stands in the truth that man's supposed quality of life is a delusion: in fact, that the world lies in the sleep of death, and is dead to its very soul. This death is total in its extent: all born of woman. And in its reign: there are no degrees in death. As saith the apostle, Rom. 5:21, Sin hath reigned unto death. That is what the work of God called quickening implies as to nature. Now,

(ii) What this implies as to consciousness

This state of death towards God, common to all born of women, implies the same absence of awareness, of consciousness, and of all sense, that is true of those laid in the grave. Just as these have passed beyond reach and communication from everyone and everything in this present world, so has the natural man, the whole world, passed beyond reach of God.

The dead moulder and decay in the grave; their flesh consumes into dust: they are under the earth, buried, eaten up of worms: they are utterly and irrevocably gone from this life and out of the world. There is no consciousness of the world they have left behind. There is no consciousness of anything on earth at all. They are gone for ever, oblivious, annihilated as to all that continues in this present world from which they have departed for ever. Just so is the whole world towards God.

With death, those means of intelligence cease to exist by which men are alerted to all that exists outside of themselves. In the grave, in a state of death, there is neither sight, hearing, taste, smell, or touch. These faculties have ceased to exist. The dead therefore cannot correspond to outward criteria, no matter what sights there are to be seen; what sounds to be heard; what things to be tasted; what aromas to be smelt; or what objects to be desired and touched: to a corpse it is all over. The means by which dead men were aware in this life of the sentient world of the living have been annihilated by death. Just so is the natural world towards God.

Life, the world, mankind, cease to exist to the dead, and the dead to all that is in time and on earth. The means of communication, of consciousness, by which the soul lived in awareness in the body, all is gone for ever: the dead are exterminated from this world of time by the death of the body. Just so is it of man towards the Eternal, who is a spirit.

But there is nothing spiritual—much less of eternity—AT ALL in man: nothing exists: he can no more communicate with, or receive communication from God, than can dead men to or from the living world. Man is spiritually dead towards God. There is absolutely no consciousness of his existence, no remote sense of the realm of his being.

No, the world, time, is one vast grave, and mankind its population of the living dead in everything that pertains towards God. Just as under the earth the grave holds vast numbers of the dead, of dead men's bones, utterly out of reach, wholly beyond the living, completely beyond consciousness, utterly incommunicable to those alive on the earth in time: so is mankind in this present world towards God. That is, God, the living God, is utterly, wholly, irrevocably beyond man's consciousness: mankind is dead to him. No means of communication exist.

Hence, all religion in the flesh, under the dead letter, the bare text of scripture, however charismatic, evangelical, fundamental, reformed, sound in divinity, on the part of natural men, in the so-called life begotten by natural birth, is utterly useless. It is all a pretence. Actual communication does not exist. Men merely pretend that it exists. In fact, nothing happens. They are dead men acting a part on the stage. BUT THERE IS NO AUDIENCE.

The natural man cannot see spiritual things, nor can he hear spiritual sounds: having ears they hear not; and as to their eyes, the god of this world has blinded their eyes: *born* blind. They are dumb: they cannot speak to God. No sounds from him reach them, and no sounds from them reach him. Their prayers are empty noises, they are neither heard nor answered.

There is no feeling of God, no consciousness of him: how could there be? They are as dead to him, as the buried dead are to them. God is a word meaning nothing; or anything; or everything: *he does not actually exist to them.* They are unconscious of him. In the spiritual realm they do not exist: but that realm is precisely where he exists: 'God is a spirit' Jn. 4:24. A spirit: utterly beyond their reach, and wholly outside of the realm of their consciousness. Spiritually mankind has no sight, no hearing, no savour, no taste, and no feeling towards God. It is impossible. THE MEANS OF COMMUNICATING WITH HIM DO NOT EXIST. Any more than the means of their communicating with the dead, or the dead with them: they are gone. Beyond reach. Outside this world, outside time, outside consciousness, beyond all rational comprehension or communication. Dead and buried.

If beyond the means of intelligence, then beyond intelligence itself. GOD IS UNKNOWN. There is no way of finding him. intelligence is utterly futile, sterile, it is useless. 'Man by wisdom knew not God.' How could man by wisdom know him to whom he is utterly dead? So the feelings. Man may profess to feel after him, but it is useless: he cannot touch him. There is no feeling in the dead. Likewise the will. Says the Saviour, 'Ye will not come to me that ye might have life.' How could they? they are dead. Dead men have no will. They cannot move. This was not only true of the Jews at the time of Jesus' coming. What was true of one is true of all. In Adam *all* die. Adam was the man, and is the man, of sin and death. And in Adam all are born. Thus death passed to all men, for that all have sinned. The whole world lies under this Fall. The whole world abideth in death. Morally and spiritually, generation by generation, by birth, the world is wholly DEAD towards God.

(iii) What this implies as to grace

First, it implies a preceding choice

The dead cannot choose. The dead cannot vote for this or that. The dead cannot elect to do one thing or another. Those in the grave can make no decision. Their committal, which was to dust, has already been made. Then nothing will do but 'LAZARUS, COME FORTH.' As well preach over the green humps of ancient graves, or cry to the stone monuments of those long dead, calling them to get up and make a decision, to make their commitment, as to mimic Christ, who alone raises the dead. It is his work, only he can do it, and whether he does it or not depends entirely upon a preceding decision, a prior election, on the part of God the Father. A preceding choice is implied: Rom. 9:16, It is not of him that willeth, nor of him that runneth, but of God that showeth mercy. I Pet. 1:2, Elect according to the foreknowledge of God the Father. Jas. 1:18, Of his own will begat he us. Jn. 1:13, Born, not of blood, nor of the will of the flesh, nor of the will of man, but of God. Jn. 15:16, Ye have not chosen me, but I have chosen you. Jn. 13:18, I know whom I have chosen. Rom. 9:23, Vessels of mercy, which God hath afore prepared unto glory. Jn. 17:6, Thine they were, and thou gavest them me. Eph. 1:4, According as he hath chosen us. Jn. 15:19, I have chosen you out of the world. Rom. 9:11, The children being not yet born, neither having done any good or evil, that the purpose of God according to election might stand, not of works, but of him that calleth. Eph. 1:4, He hath chosen us in him before the foundation of the world. Eph. 1:5, Having predestinated us unto the adoption of children by Jesus Christ to himself, according to the good pleasure of his will.

Here is a preceding choice with a witness, and a will to choose indeed: the choice is all of God, and his will, exercised in choice, was determined before the foundation of the world, before the creation of Adam, and before the existence of the Fall. And where is the will of man in that? That is, always provided that dead men in the grave *could* will. All that man ever willed, and once willed, was to sin and die. What God willed, according to his own counsel, was to quicken into life. But he will quicken whom he will quicken, he will have mercy on whom he will have mercy, and whom he will, he will harden. No less than this is implied in grace.

Next, it implies a preceding work

No work of quickening can take place in the sinner, while the law of God thunders against that sinner; while the curse of the law still sounds its terrible indictment in a ministration of death; while offended justice remains unappeased; while sins mount up to heaven unatoned; or while the righteousness of God still remains without vindication, the vengeance of heaven without satisfaction, and the wrath to come, pregnant with fiery indignation, abides unexecuted. Before any recovery can be made, before any quickening can take place, A SUITED SACRIFICE MUST BE FOUND, FULL PAYMENT MUST BE RENDERED, AND A SUBSTITUTIONARY ATONEMENT MUST BE PROVIDED. No quickening, no interior work, could possibly occur WITHOUT THIS PRIOR SATISFACTION, or in the special case of the old testament saints, without its being seen in the counsels of God as certain to be accomplished.

A foundation of perfect atonement, particularly and precisely made for the very sinner who is to be quickened, must have taken place exterior to that sinner, and on his behalf, before ever a holy God could approach the condemned man. An external substitutionary sacrifice, made on the sinner's behalf before in time, must precede any internal deliverance at present in the soul. Such a quickening within must be RIGHT, and SEEN to be right, lawfully to deliver the soul from death. His debt *must have been paid*; his sins *must have been covered*; the wrath of God *must have been propitiated*; the law *must have been upheld*; the curse *must have been executed*; justice *must have been vindicated*; and divine righteousness *must have been satisfied*. Deliverance cannot be at the expense of justice. Full atonement, and that by blood, must have been made in the death of the substitute for that very soul in particular, beforehand, so that in consequence that same soul might be quickened thereafter. There must have been a particular preceding exterior work.

Last, it implies preceding stages in the Spirit's work

If quickening is the fourth stage, and we have seen that it is the fourth stage, by which the grace of God brings a dead sinner to saving faith, it follows that three preceding stages are implied. These prior stages were those in which by the interior work of the Spirit sinners were brought to feel their state before God. They felt the blast of the trumpet sounding in the sepulchre of their souls: the trump stirred the dust, shook the bones, and alerted the slumbering soul.

Raised up by the sound of the alarm, the alerted sinner, appalled at his state, to which he had been utterly oblivious, supposing his dreams were the actuality, now shaken and trembling, cries out at his awakening. The terrors of death; the fear of wrath; the awareness of the indignation of the Almighty; the consciousness of the dead, hopeless, helpless state of his soul; the inexorability of the law; the inescapability of the curse: all these press in upon the newly awakened sinner, whereas just before dreams of carnal ease and worldly security had lulled him to sleep as he looked forward to a loving God and a wondrous heaven. No more!

No more: as blind Bartimaeus cried out, he cries out; as men tried in vain to quiet Bartimaeus, so men strive in vain to quiet the awakened sinner: he knows he is awake, he knows he had been dreaming in the sleep of death, and, awakened, now he cries out in terror. Then, sinners who are to be quickened, had before been awakened; they feel their state by a preceding work: and if they feel it, then they are awake. If they cried out, then they were alarmed. And if, as abased and humbled to the dust, they begged for pardon, then were they convicted indeed. HENCE, a preceding work is implied by which they come to Christ that they might have life.

II. Consider, secondly, THE MEANING OF QUICKENING

(i) The meaning of the root

The word used for quickening in the new testament is a Greek compound, to all intents and purposes the compounding together of a noun and a verb, making one word. It is in the noun part of this compound that the root is seen. It is the word for LIFE. But it is not the only Greek new testament word for life. There are in fact three distinct new testament Greek words indiscriminately rendered 'life' in the English bible. Consider:

> 1. *PSUCHĒ* (pronounced PSY-KEY) As in 'psychic'. This word means 'breath', or 'breathing', and is the SIGN of life. So when a mirror is placed over the mouth of a person apparently dead, and misting occurs, it is evident that his breath is still in him. He is yet alive. Breathing signifies that he is not dead, whatever the appearances. It is the SIGN of life.

> 2. *BIOS* (pronounced BI-OHS) As in 'biology'. This indicates the mode, means, qualities, span, the attributes of life. In fact it describes the EFFECT of life. It is the EFFECT of life, it lives THUS; as opposed to the sign of life, it breathes thus.

> 3. *ZOŌ* (pronounced ZOO-OH) As in 'zoology'. This word is indicative of the quick motions of life, its moving quality, its aliveness, its quickness, its swarming movement. It is the ESSENCE of life, it points to life in its very ESSENCE.

The nature of the word, QUICK, as in QUICKENING, when measured against these three Greek words all meaning life in one form or another, immediately shows which of the three provides the noun part of the Greek compound translated QUICKENING. It is ZOŌ (zoo-oh) life in its very ESSENCE, its aliveness, the seething motion that is life, its self-generative quickness: the very ESSENCE OF LIFE.

Now to the noun ZOŌ has been added the verb *POIEŌ* (poy-oh) so as to form the compound translated QUICKENING. The verb *POIEŌ* (poy-oh) means 'to make'; 'to do'; 'to fashion'; 'to work'; even 'to create'. When used in relation to LIFE, the reference must be to the Creator, God withal, who made, created, life by his word and the breath of his lips. Thus the word QUICKENING indicates the prerogative of the deity.

The compound is formed by joining ZOŌ with *POIEŌ* giving a new word, that is, ZOŌPOIEŌ (zoo-oh-poy-oh), meaning, TO MAKE ALIVE; TO CREATE LIFE; in one word, TO QUICKEN.

(ii) The meaning of the word

The word QUICKENING describes a work, though done in the body, which goes far deeper than the body. This work of God penetrates far beyond the faculties of the intellect, it is vastly more than the illumination of the mind, than the inshining of the beams of God's glory into the understanding. It is deeper even than the revelation of the Spirit to the inner man: all these things are effected by the light of God: they correspond to revelation or inshining from the rays that beam from God's glory to the inward man. But QUICKENING is more than that.

Moreover, QUICKENING describes a work deeper than the effect of the presence of God himself, considered as acting only upon the emotions, or as exciting the affections, or simply as stirring the deepest passions of devotion: for QUICKENING IS much more than that which the life of God EFFECTS, or the IMPRESSIONS that this brings, in man. Quickening is more than the effect of the life of God upon the will, the volition, the intention or resolution governing the soul. The presence of God may affect the will, the volition, and affect it profoundly, BUT THE NAME OF THE BEING AFFECTED, the result of such impressions, is NOT QUICKENING. Quickening is more than that, though multitudes, one could say today almost all, trust in a delusion of being saved by far, far less than this. Had they all of these things, STILL THEY WOULD BE SHORT OF QUICKENING.

Then, QUICKENING is not the result of light from God, it is not illumination, nor is it revelation: neither yet is QUICKENING the result of impressions, influences, even from the life of God itself, deep as these may go. All these things are short of the depth to which quickening goes. QUICKENING is the IMPARTING OF THAT LIFE ITSELF, SO THAT IT, IN ITSELF, IS GENERATED IN THE INNERMOST SPIRIT, THERE TO ABIDE FOR EVER. Quickening IMPLANTS life, rather than being merely the effect of the life of God upon the soul and its faculties. It is not an effect, not an impression, not an influence: IT IS A NEW CREATION. Life is communicated so as to be generated deeper even than the soul, even in the innermost spirit within the being of man. And, once generated, it abides for ever.

Hence the word means a work more profound than anything done in or to the soul itself, beyond the faculties, propensities, qualities, or attributes of the soul: quickening is deeper than a work in the soul. Indeed, it is even deeper, even more profound, than the life in the soul, and of the soul: it is not that one's life is influenced: it is deeper than that. It involves much more than that God should act upon the soul, or in the life of the soul. *It is not to quicken that life.* For that life—in its fashion, deathly as it is—is quick by nature already.

To quicken, which is God's prerogative, is to create in depths beyond both the soul and the life generated by nature, a new, utterly new, spiritual life; and a new, utterly new, spiritual nature, *not in existence before this work took place*. It is to generate in the spirit in the inmost man another kind of life than that which exists in human nature, to create a life within, other than that with which one was born. THAT IS TO QUICKEN: TO CREATE LIFE WITHIN, NEVER IN EXISTENCE BEFORE.

(iii) The meaning of the life

First, it is variously described

That life by which sinners are quickened is variously described so as to clarify the meaning, as follows:

It is described as ETERNAL life. This is utterly different in nature and essence from the life of man. The life of which the soul of man is possessed is immortal. Hence the death of the body does not terminate it: that is the nature of immortality. It never ends. But it did begin, by generation, at conception. Practically, it begins in this world at birth and lives out its span in time. After death, the death of the body, disembodied, it awaits the resurrection of that great last day, and the judgment to come.

But, John 3:15, *eternal life* is not so: *it was never created*. By definition, being *eternal*, it had no beginning. The very fact that it never began indicates a difference in essence and nature from the life of man. *Eternal life* is proper to God alone, and is utterly different from human life, being divine in its nature, and eternal in its duration. *That* is what is quickened in the heart of the sinner.

Jn. 3:36, It is EVERLASTING LIFE. It lasts for ever, cannot begin, age, fade, tire or end. It is not subject to age, or the ages, to the world, to time, or to eternity. It IS. I AM THAT I AM rings everlastingly from eternity to eternity, as fresh and quick in the eternal ages to come as it ever was in that endless eternity which is past. It is, it was, and it ever shall be, divine and everlasting within itself.

Jn. 5:26, It is THE LIFE OF THE FATHER AND THE SON. As the Father hath life in himself, so hath he given to the Son to have life in himself. It is GOD's life, that which is unique to the deity, the three divine Persons in the Godhead, the life of *Father, Son, and Holy Ghost*. It is that life, *that* life, which is quickened in the sinner.

It is THE BREAD OF LIFE, because as food, taken from outside of oneself into the mouth, is assimilated into the system—or one starves and dies of hunger—so it is with eternal life. The bread of life, quickening the inward spirit of a man, is absorbed into the life of the soul, in union, assimilated into all the faculties from within, so giving nourishment and energy even as bread does to the body.

It is THE WORD OF LIFE, Jn. 6:63, proceeding from the mouth of Christ with authority to command all whom he chooses into spiritual life, and spiritual life into them.

This life is described as NEWNESS OF LIFE, Rom. 6:4. New: there never was anything like this before, it never came from human nature, natural generation, the seed of man, flesh and blood, or from the womb. Neither did this newness of life come from divine illumination, revelation, gifts, impressions of the Spirit, or any work, as such, any work of God wrought upon the soul. It is a new creation, a hitherto unexperienced generation of life, the quickening of *newness* of life, thence for evermore to abide in the hidden man of the heart.

It is called THE SPIRIT OF LIFE, Rom. 8:2,6,10, in that although it infuses the life, floods the soul, indwells the heart, what is quickened has its seat in the spirit of man, separate from all, in a new, interior, spiritual existence. The Spirit of life fills the soul, but is distinct from it, deeper than it, creating within a

40

realm, faculty, an enlargement of the spirit never there before, rendering one spiritual, dependent upon the supply of the Spirit, and aware thereby of an entirely new generation, realm, and divinity, of which hitherto one had been oblivious.

Eph. 4:18, It is the LIFE OF GOD. Not of man, but *in* man. Another life, divine life, God's life, quickening within the life of man, so that another order of manhood is formed by this indwelling life of God.

Col. 3:3, It is a HIDDEN LIFE. It is invisible, inaudible, intangible, it is of the heart, in the inner man, mysterious, hidden, beyond the reach of senses, past the comprehension of reason. Men will not own what it is, nor believe it, unless they possess it, 'Therefore the world knoweth us not, because it knew him not.' Men, the world, will only admit that their *own* life has become religious. Not so with the quickened: hidden, inward, deep down and beyond the soul, the hidden life of God in Christ is quickened within us, the hope of glory.

I Pet. 3:7, It is described as THE GRACE OF LIFE. Absolutely free, unbidden, untaken, unconditional, this seed of the tree of life planted by the Prince of life, quickened by the living God, filled with the Spirit of life, watered by the water of life, is all of grace. It is all of God, this is the true God and eternal life, God has planted this grace of life by the hands of his own Son, it is of his own will, not ours, ours is nothing to do with it, he chose to do it, and he did do it of his own will, not consulting or telling us of his matters, but we awake to find ourselves in his likeness, crying, Grace, grace, unto it: it is the grace of life, and life more abundant.

Next, as to the meaning of the life,

It is graphically described

For example:

      In Jn. 1. As the baptism of the Holy Ghost;
      In Jn. 2. As water turned into wine;

41

In Jn. 3. As being born from above;
In Jn. 4. As a well of water springing up into everlasting life;
In Jn. 5. As life from the dead;
In Jn. 6. As bread from heaven;
In Jn. 7. As rivers of living water;
In Jn. 8. As justification unto life;
In Jn. 9. As sight to the blind;
In Jn. 10. As the life of the elect sheep of the heavenly shepherd;
In Jn. 11. As the resurrection and the life;
In Jn. 12. As a corn of wheat, falling into the ground and dying, thereafter bearing much fruit;
In Jn. 13. As being washed of God by the hands of his Son;
In Jn. 14. As dwelling in the Father and the Son by one Spirit;
In Jn. 15. As being fruitful branches in the heavenly vine;
In Jn. 16. As being not of the world, but chosen out of the world;
In Jn. 17. As being given by the Father to the Son from eternity, to dwell in God to everlasting;
In Jn. 18. As seeing the Son standing and overcoming, amidst a world fallen and overcome;
In Jn. 19. As beholding the blood and water flowing from the side of the crucified Saviour;
In Jn. 20. As being breathed upon by the risen Son to receive the Holy Ghost;
In Jn. 21. As beholding his power and glory, full of grace and truth.

Lastly, it is comparatively described

Compared with water, food, a springing well, bread, rivers of living water, wine, life from the dead, a blowing wind, many and various are the figures used to describe QUICKENING and the life which ensues.

Just so in the case of that with which it is contrasted. The quickening of life is set in opposition to the dead letter, dry forms, outward ceremonies, human traditions, carnal ordinances, a legal ministry, the ministration of death, and all worldly religion. It is set against every form of human enthusiasm or rational dogmatising that merely describes Jesus Christ, or does no more than point to him as being the Lamb of God which taketh away the sin of the world, without his being formed within. It is as opposed to all that falls short of the sprinkling of the blood upon the soul by the hand of the Lord himself, and the eating of his body and the drinking of his blood in the interior experience of the quickened soul.

Compared with baptism, quickening is described as being immersed in the river of the water of life, as being made to drink into one Spirit. It is like the outpouring of water, poured over and into the soul as from the great heights of the ascended glory, by the Son of God; it is like being filled with the Spirit, in a word, IT IS THE BAPTISM OF THE HOLY GHOST.

Described in relation to the ravages of time, it is immortal life; in respect of the corrupting rot of decay, it is life from the dead; in relation to worldly, earthly, carnal life, it is called eternal life; with regard to the natural man working for life out of the scriptures, it is called, newness of life; and in relation to the dust of death, the stillness and gloom of the grave, it is EVERLASTING LIFE.

When the life that is in the Father and the Son, by which sinners are quickened, is compared with the generation which springs from Adam, the man of sin and death, by way of father and mother, that is, carnal life conceived of his seed in

43

her womb, then that divine, eternal life is called God's seed, which remaineth in one for ever, being of that birth named REGENERATION.

Described with regard to parents, wife, children, husband, brethren, and sisters, yea, and one's own life also; all natural relations, national ties, and all that pertains to the first man Adam, the law, and this present age and world; quickening is seen in relation to an eternal election before time began, belonging to an everlasting glory that shall abide when time is no more. It is of the last Adam, the second man, pertaining to sonship, and to what is called the adoption of children. Moreover this quickening is above all, being beyond the natural life, the process of decay and death marked by birthdays, together with all that is born of the flesh: it is to be BORN AGAIN.

In contrast with this present age, the world that now is, the birth that proceeds from and all that is generated by the man of this world, yea, all the nations, all civilisation, all that is in the world, and the whole of this age, or time, all human achievement, earthly glory, all that is from beneath, up from man, then it is BORN FROM ABOVE.

Described in respect of all religion that ever went before, Moses, the law, the legal rule, the commandments, conditional promises, works, the dead letter, the traditions of the fathers, historical theology, religious learning, fundamentalist Pharisees, scriptural scribes, worldly Herodians, divinity doctors, ceremonialist performers, traditionalist elders, hierarchical priests, and all of God's religion taken up by man in Adam, all the bible religiously followed by men in the flesh, all the gospel zealously embraced in the carnal mind and affections, all the soft sentimental or hard doctrinal pointing to Jesus, it is to be born ANEW. *Not born before!*

When regarded in the light of religious exercises, whether public or private, whether in the means of grace, as men say, the services, preaching, public prayer; or whether in solitary religion, prayer in the closet, private reading, the giving of alms, fasting or self-denial, the meditation and study of the word of God, the mortification or humbling of the soul, the instruction of the mind, the flowing of the affections, religious exercise of will: all that is either exterior to the body; or interior in the flesh; all that is out of oneself towards God, the exercises of the natural soul to Godward, all is set in opposition to Quickening. God purposes a quickening, whilst as yet man is dead, blind, and unconscious of him and his work. And God does it, the whole thing is of him, and in the deepest spirit, where nothing was before. From this inwardness of life, from this depth of quickening, flows out the only religion, the sole religious exercise, pleasing to him by Jesus Christ. Now this inward work, as opposed to all outward exercise, is to be BORN OF THE SPIRIT.

In these ways, by such analogies and contrasts, QUICKENING is VARIOUSLY DESCRIBED; GRAPHICALLY DESCRIBED; and is COMPARATIVELY DESCRIBED. Comparatively described, that is, as being spiritually compatible with that event, when, once life is conceived, after nine long months shut up in the womb, following the hours of travail and the minutes of anguished labour, a new, hitherto non-existent, unique being enters into the world of self-existence: a child is born. WITH THIS, QUICKENING IS COMPARABLE.

CONVERSION

V

Conversion

5. CONVERSION

I. THE MEANING OF CONVERSION

(i) The meaning of the English

This is a word of Latin origin which entered the English language via the Old French, going back to the fifteen hundreds in its recorded use. It means:

Rotation, 1726; Turning 1712; Returning 1682 (Transposition or Inversion in Logic 1551. In Law, The action of wrongfully converting something to one's own use, 1615.)

II. The action of converting or fact of being converted to a religion, a belief, or an opinion, *specifically*, to Christianity, (Middle English).

2. Theologically. The turning of sinners to God, a spiritual change from sinfulness to a religious life.

3. A change of form or properties, condition or function, 1549. Hence in many technical uses in *manufacture*. Militarily, *conversion* is the change of front to a flank.

III. Translation: a translation, version, 1653.

2. Mathematically, change of a number or quantity into another denomination, 1557.

3. Substitute or change for something else.

CONVERT is defined as:
to turn about, direct, to turn back, to invert, transpose (from 1551). In Logic, to transpose the terms of a proposition by conversion. To reverse the course of, to the opposite or contrary.

II. To turn in mind, feeling, or conduct, 1557, to turn from a course of conduct. To cause to turn to a religion, belief, or opinion.

(ii) The meaning of the Latin

From the word VERTŌ, 'turn', plus the preposition CON, 'against', comes the Latin verb CONVERTERE: 'to turn against', *.. to make to turn completely round or back* ('against the direction in which one had been going'). To turn completely. To change completely, transform. To turn intently (in a certain direction) *direct* to an object. Also used in Latin (as an application). To translate, i.e., to turn from one language into another.

(iii) The meaning of the Greek

From the verb STREPHŌ, 'to turn', plus the preposition EPI, 'upon', 'on', comes the Greek compound EPISTREPHŌ, 'to turn on, or upon', in the sense of 'around', 'back', or to 'return', 'turn to someone'. 'Turn on a pivot', 'return to a source', 'wheel about', 'convert'. To turn upon the direction in which one was going, as on a pivot, to face the opposite way.

(iv) The meaning of the Hebrew

There are two Hebrew words which give the sense, and the root, of conversion in the mind of the Spirit and the word of the LORD:

I. *HAPHAK*; 'Turn', 'overturn', 'turn about', 'change', 'transform', 'change into', 'reverse', 'be upturned'.

II. *SHUB*; 'Turn back', 'return', 'go back', especially 'return unto', 'come back.'

In I, *HAPHAK*, the emphasis is on the revolution of the turn; with II, *SHUB*, it is upon the ultimate, returning, direction of the turn. Both words are fulfilled in the new testament conception of CONVERSION. (I) It is a *radical* revolution; and (II) It is a *reverse* direction, so as to progress in a line directly opposite to the previous course.

New testament conversion therefore involves three things: First, it involves a *radical* revolution or turn; Second, it involves making *progress*, taking a *course*, actually *proceeding* in the new direction faced as a result of turning; Third, it involves both turning and proceeding being done *immediately*. It is *abrupt*: *sudden*. The thing is done, and done thoroughly, radically, *instantly*.

II. THE NATURE OF CONVERSION

(i) It is first passive

That is, GOD does it. Not the sinner. Whatever the sinner may do, it is nothing but a consequence of God's initiative: THE WORK IS OF GOD.

Before ever coming near to the work of Conversion, the word of God had sounded an alarm within the soul of the sinner. This was not the bare text or letter. God spoke by it. His voice, as the sound of a trumpet, sounded.

Thus the sinner was awakened. This was effected by the sound of God's voice in the word coming with interior power much as does the great blast of a trumpet upon the ears.

51

As a result of waking up things are seen. One is awakened from deadly sleep, from delusive dreams, and one sees things as they really are: This is not now the result of sound, but of light from God. His presence appears in a terrible light, full of wrath and fiery indignation. His law becomes a ministry of condemnation, the curse appearing dreadful and immutable with it, against sins one did not dream of until the terrible reality of this LIGHT shone in upon one. Wrath is revealed from heaven, sin, inbred sin, is revealed within, darkness and despair appear without: this is to be awake, to see the light.

The light shines through, rather than upon, the outward actions, the very best of which now appear hypocritical and polluted. Inward intentions are illuminated, all of which come to light as stained, soiled, full of self, pride, lust, covetousness, anger, yet so guileful, lying, false and deceitful in the outward appearance. Ever deeper shines the light, even to the bottom of the heart, upon the settled direction, the resolution of the inmost volition governing the course of the soul. This is seen to be wholly motivated by self-interest. It is entirely selfish. It is as contrary to the love of God as contrary can be. The whole body is full of darkness: not the fruit only, the tree is evil; it is the root that is rotten. Such piercing beams of light utterly convict the soul. It lies prostrate, helpless, self-condemned yet God-justifying. Now damnation is seen not only as clearly real: it is seen to be utterly just.

After this the mercy of God—for, clean contrary to what the condemned sinner supposes, all is mercy—appears in a new way. For the first time the mercy of God appears in a way of life. Not of sound; nor of sight. That is, not by his voice; nor by his light. But of quickening. That is, by his divine, everlasting life. Now, from this, and only from this, and not until this, comes the power, the energy of life, by which God inwardly turns the sinner. This turning is called CONVERSION, and, of necessity, God does it all. All poor, and even quickened, sinners can cry is this: 'Turn us again, O God, and cause thy face to shine; and we shall be saved.' 'Draw us, we will run after thee.' Though quickened, yet all the life, and all the power, is the Lord's. The sinner is passive. It is God who is active. When he acts, and only then; when he turns the sinner, and not until he turns the sinner; conversion takes place, and poor lost souls turn unto God. First, passive.

It is not something we do of ourselves. But it is something God does to us within ourselves. We *are* converted: we do not convert ourselves: by definition another does it to us. That is, we are passive: it is God that is active: *he* turns us.

If so, if the initiative is God's, if we are passive, there were reasons in God for converting us, not to be found in ourselves. It is not of works. It is not because of religious virtue. It is not grounded in any inclination towards God, to religion, to be saved, on the part of those to be converted, not found in those who are not converted. All the reasons for God converting us, are to be found in him, and found in him before he actually exerted his power and initiative to do it. Therefore it is not only an act of the power of God, in which we are passive, but also a decision of the initiative of God before so acting, thus to act. Hence conversion answers to a previous determination:

FIRSTLY, OF THE FATHER; 'JACOB have I loved.' 'Ye were as SHEEP going astray.' 'Ye lay in your blood, and I SAID, Live.' 'When THE LORD turned again the captivity of Zion.'

ALSO, OF THE SON; 'When', said he to Peter, 'thou art converted'; this is 'the ransomed of the Lord RETURNING', and 'the redeemed of the Lord shall TURN.' If not, HE blinds their eyes, and hardens their hearts 'Lest', saith Jesus, 'they should be converted, and I should heal them.' For, saith he, 'Except ye

BE converted'—not convert yourselves: except HE should do it, and YE should BE it—'and become as little children, ye shall in no case enter into the kingdom of heaven.' But all this stands in his prerogative, power, and decision.

LIKEWISE, OF THE HOLY SPIRIT; Before ever coming to conversion, in those who are to be converted, it has been shown, an alarm must first be sounded; sinners must be awakened; conviction must follow; quickening must take place: and it does, as surely as day follows night. And wherefore? Because it is the divine Person of the Holy Ghost who brings in these mighty operations of God upon those who are to be converted. This is called, in sum, 'The washing of regeneration, and renewing of the Holy Ghost.'

And as regenerate, as the quickening effects of life in the Holy Ghost flow out in the soul, this wonderful indwelling of life, issuing forth in the work of the living God, turns right about-face the whole inward man: the name given to that turning is, conversion.

The soul is converted, in consequence of its being quickened. It is the life, energy, and power of that quickening, surging up irresistibly through the soul, that turns one. That is, the soul turns—STREPHŌ—upon this—EPI. It is the active work of God. It turns upon this point. It is all of God. The soul is passive. It happens TO the soul. The soul does not do it, God does it, and in consequence of what God does, the soul is turned.

Thus our heart language is 'Turn us, O God of our salvation', Psalm 85. Again, Isa. 49, 'He restoreth the preserved of Israel', and, Psalm 23, 'He restoreth my soul', where 'restore' is *SHUB*, 'to turn back', 'return from the opposite direction'. Hence the power of the Holy Ghost upon John's ministry effects this: 'Many of the children of Israel shall HE turn', Lk. 1:16. Where the Spirit by the word effects the turning, in consequence of which Israel is turned, answering the helpless plea 'Turn us again, O God, and cause thy face to shine; and we shall be saved', Psalm 80:3. Hence, Rom. 11:26, 'HE shall turn away ungodliness from Jacob.' And the power of the Holy Ghost in Paul's gospel is such that he should: 'turn them from darkness to light, and from the power of Satan unto God'—HE should turn THEM. For how could those in such a strait turn themselves?—And, being turned, it then follows 'that they may receive forgiveness of sins', Acts 26:18. This is 'conversion', and it is all God's activity. The soul is passive, but acted upon from within, out of the quickened Spirit, to turn it right about-face from the inside out, through 180°. I say, This is conversion.

(ii) It is then active

That is, the alarmed, awakened, convicted, and quickened soul is moved of God, by turning it, TO TURN. The soul says, 'Turn us, and we shall be turned.' The turning which God effects is not co-operative, as though the Almighty needed the help of the soul. But it is not coercive, as though it were forced upon a reluctant soul. That turning without which even the quickened soul cannot be turned, makes the soul long to turn, eager to convert, it cries, 'Draw us, we will run after thee'; there is, in the quickened soul, Jer. 44:14, 'A desire to return.'

Hence, as turned by the activity of God, the quickened soul, in and of itself passive, being unequal to the work, though crying for it, answers in joyful response to the converting, turning power of God welling up in life from the inward man through every part. Thus it appears that it is God that works in the soul both *to will* and *to do* of his good pleasure.

So the Spirit draws, and Christ calls, and the Father moves, the quickened soul, TO BE CONVERTED. GOD AND THE FATHER works all in all, as THE SPIRIT surges up from within, and THE SON calls down from above. By this calling of Christ, in harmony with the life of the Spirit, and the inworking of

God and the Father, the entire heavenly gift of grace conspires with each divine work to effect the whole.

The calling of Christ plays a mighty, indispensable part in the conversion of a sinner quickened by the Spirit of life. In this work one's name is sweetly whispered by the voice of the Son of God in the heavenly glory, mysteriously echoing in the inward parts of the soul below. Immediately, at the voice of the Son of God above, the Spirit wells up through the soul beneath, and the power of God makes the inmost being to tremble with joy at the sound of jubilee.

Then one's old chains, yokes, shackles, bonds, bands, grave-clothes and shrouds of death, lie cast off and scattered in the dust. The iron bars are rent in twain, the gates of brass burst asunder, the prison doors swing open of their own accord, and, as life surges up through the old dead body of the helpless prisoner, a great cry resounds and echoes through the vaults of the prison-house: 'LAZARUS, COME FORTH!' The soul knows its name, knows it has been spoken, knows it has been spoken at an irresistible time of calling, and knows whose voice this is: 'My sheep hear my voice, and I know them, and they follow me.'

Thus, Acts 11, 'They believed and turned to the Lord', and, being both moved and called, they answered when 'Paul preached that they should repent and turn to God', Acts 26, likewise responding from within by the work of God to Peter's cry, 'Repent ye, and be converted'. Indeed, at this mighty work of God, it is evident, 'Ye turned to God from idols', I Thess. 1:9.

III. THE WORK OF CONVERSION

(i) It is radical

First, in time

It is radical, this work of Conversion, in terms of TIME. It is SUDDEN. It must be sudden. It is invariably sudden. You don't grow into it. You turn into it. You are not born into it. You are reborn into it. It is not imperceptible. It is unmistakable. So Paul on the Damascus road. So the calling of Peter, James, John, Matthew, and the other disciples. 'Follow me', said Jesus: and they turned right round, and followed him. 'Ye turned from idols.'

This, in every case, and all cases, was radical, instantaneous, and sudden. If a birth is imperceptible and takes innumerable years to materialise, it is no baby that is born. Nothing but gas and air. In all cases, and every instance, the procedure follows the same pattern of stages, and the same period of time, so that after some nine months, labour begins, travail commences, and, suddenly, a baby is born into the world. And, 'Except ye be converted and become as babes, ye cannot enter into the kingdom.' One is quickened to it. And birth, at the end of nine months, is sudden. And to be converted; after having been first alarmed, then awakened, followed by conviction, next quickened, I say, it follows, of necessity, that conversion comes to the birth. And the birth is radical in terms of time: it is sudden, unmistakable.

For, 'Ye must be born again.' And the birth, when it comes, when the life within bursts forth, appears suddenly and unmistakably. It is a definite, an unmistakable, an astonishing event in point of time. The quickening of life preceded, but the turning, the conversion, the bursting out of life to turn round the whole soul, followed. This turning, this radical, sudden conversion is described as, and compared to:

In Lev. the turning of the hair white (from black!). Job 28, Overturning the mountains by the roots. Psalm 30, Turning mourning into dancing. Neh. 13, Turning the curse into a blessing. Ex. 7, Turning a rod into a serpent. Psalm 66, Turning the sea into dry land. Psalm 78, Turning rivers into blood. Psalm 32, Turning moisture into drought. Psalm 114, Turning the rock into a standing water, the flint into a fountain of waters. Isa. 29, Turning things upside down. Isa. 34, Turning streams of water into pitch, and Joel 2, Turning the sun into darkness, and the moon into blood.

Thus the work of conversion, as it appears in the use of the word, and the employment of figures, is, firstly, radical: It is radical in point of time. This we have seen: observe next, however, that it is

Radical in degree

The work of conversion is radical in degree. Why? Because the amount of turn demanded by new testament conversion is one hundred and eighty degrees! It is a 180° turn FROM this TO that. Here is no 2° 'Committal'. This is not a 0.5° 'Accepting Jesus'. It is no 0.005° 'Letting him into your heart.' Here is no 1.2° 'Thinking things through'; no 0.1° 'Theological viewpoint'. No 0.001° 'Fundamentalist stand', nor is it a 0.0° 'Reformed position', much less a dead stop Calvinistic burial service. Neither yet is it the sinking subsidence of a Charismatic delusion. No, IT IS A 180°, 100% CONVERSION!

Salvation, Saving faith, bears no resemblance to what is called today 'believing', by which modern evangelicals mean sentimental assent held in isolation from any preceding work of God in the soul, or from heaven-sent preaching, or from any doctrine of the gospel. Conversion is certainly not the modern evangelical substitute for believing, namely, being persuaded in the flesh. Nor is it even or only genuinely believing, in itself alone considered: it is doing so AS CONVERTED! The soul has been alarmed, awakened, convicted, quickened, and so converted, and is *thus* brought to saving faith, and at that, by way of repentance towards God. CONVERTED, *turned*, quickened souls are those brought to believe. All the rest, which is nearly all one sees in current evangelicalism, denominationalism, the charismatic delusion, the reformed act, Protestantism, fundamentalism, and Christendom in general, all the rest, I say, is easy-believing false faith.

How little we hear of the work of the Spirit in and before Conversion. This apostasy came in with the sin of our fore-fathers. It was vastly accelerated by that man Spurgeon, together with all the American mass evangelists, so-called, Arminians every one, such as his friend Moody, and other like opportunists. It was greatly helped by the Brethren movement, led by J.N. Darby and others, Arminian easy-believers all, with the perfidious Open Brethren departure even more full of free-willing, light-as-air, man-pleasing, dead-letter, outward form, text professors. I say, how little we hear today of a 180° turning, a change of course that is radical in time, in degree, in the inner man, surging up in divine life effecting the conversion of the alarmed, awakened, convicted and quickened soul.

But where do we hear of this now, much less see the evidence of it? Indeed, how little we even hear the word CONVERSION. It is all socio-psychological tripe, the trash of hip-educated opportunists, of community concepts, psychological notions, or else it is all 'practicing' Christians, whatever that means, or else committed 'believers', as they say, but not alarmed, awakened, convicted, quickened, converted sinners, now called saints, the work in whom stands in the power of the Holy Ghost, the inworking of God the Father, and the living word of the Son of God. They know nothing, these Arminians, that fill the sects, denominations, gospel halls, Brethren Assemblies, and 'churches', *nothing* of the power of Almighty God in salvation, and hence, *nothing of the true gospel*. Not so the early church:

Then it was, Mt. 18, '*except* ye be converted ye cannot enter into the kingdom.' And again, Acts 3:19, 'Repent ye and *be converted*'. The power of God went forth, Acts 3:26, '*in turning* every one of you *away* from his sins.' Hence the apostle by the power of the Holy Ghost could, Acts 15:3, 'Declare unto you the *conversion* of the Gentiles'. Because, without exception, Acts 14:15, 'We preach unto you that ye *should turn*', which is what you shall never do without *the doctrine* of the gospel in the mouth of the sent ministers of Christ, as it was in the beginning; and the *power* of the Holy Ghost, having first alarmed, then awakened, next convicted, afterwards quickened, *and so converted* all who are to be brought to *saving faith*, that is, even as many as the Lord our God shall call—as opposed to as many as fleshly pretenders deceive—as many as the Lord our God shall call, namely, all who are ordained to eternal life: 'For as many as were ordained to eternal life believed', and none other, Acts 13:48.

Now this turning, radical in degree, observe, IS FIRST NEGAT-IVE: IT IS TO TURN *FROM*

Turn from what?

For example, turn from the world, from all worldliness, and from all worldly diversions, sporting, and entertainment. Conversion is not IN the world, or IN worldliness, it is FROM the world, and OUT OF worldliness. 'Love not the world, neither the things that are in the world.' Friendship with the world is enmity against God. Then, the converted man surely turns from it, for, 'If any man love the world, the love of the Father is not in him.' Again, conversion is not IN the flesh, it is FROM the flesh, with all its attendant lusts. 'But ye are not in the flesh, but in the Spirit', and the reason is, ye have turned from the one to the other. Then how many modern evangelicals are converted? It is 'turn FROM idols', not towards them. It is turn FROM ignorance, not into it.

Conversion is not to carry on as one was before, but to turn from the way in which one carried on before. And it is not to turn from SOME things, but ALL things. Not in mind and conduct only, but in heart and soul also, and, indeed, prim-arily, for it is to turn *from the heart.* 'Rend your heart, and not your garments.'

How corrupted this is today, as with all the doctrine! How spurious, worldly, and unchanged are our modern professors of religion! How different it was in days gone by! How different it was in the beginning. THEN, they turned from:

II Chron. 36, A hard heart. Neh. 9, Wicked works in religion. Psalm 51, Joyless religion. II Chron. 7, 'All thy wickedness'. Lev. 6, Dishonest business. Ruth 1, Moabite or worldly mindedness. Jer. 3, Backsliding. Jer. 5, Obstinacy. Jer. 8, Deceitful pretence. Jer. 18, Every one from his evil way. Hos. 7, From false returning: 'They returned, but *not to the most High.*' Joel 2, From the old ways of dead and false religion. Mal. 3, From evasion, 'Ye said, Wherein shall we return?' Ezek. 14, From your idols. Ezek. 14, again, From *all* your sins. Ezek. 30, From *all* your transgressions. Psalm 78, From tempting God. Psalm 85, From foolishness. II Chron. 7, From forsaking God's statutes. Gal. 4, From weak and beggarly elements. I Thes. 1, From idols. Acts 3, From your sins. Rom. 11, From ungodliness. II Tim. 1, From those professing Christ with their mouths, whilst turning against his ministers in their hearts. Heb. 12, From those who refused to hear him, that is, the Son of God, who speaketh from heaven. Eph. 4:22, From the former conversation or mode of spending time, such as so-called holidays, and 'leisure', as men call it. *That is, they turned from all idols; from all carnality; from the world, and all worldliness; all neglect of the bible, of prayer, of the company of God's people; all refusal to hear the word of God; all denial of authority in the ministry and in the ecclesia; all disorderly, presumptuous, or unrighteous conduct.* Just as their women turned from *all worldly dress, outward show and cosmetic appearance, as well as from an upstart spirit.*

And they turned from the heart, wholeheartedly, joyfully, gladly, totally, and irrevocably, burning their bridges behind them, so as to make it IMPOSSIBLE to return, thus manifesting a sound conversion in the sight of God, and before all men.

Further, this turning, radical in degree, which is first negative —that is, it is to turn *from*—is ALSO POSITIVE: IT IS TO TURN *TO*

Turn to what?

For example, 'they turned *to* God from idols'. They did not only turn from idols. They were not simply negative. They did not only protest. They were not mere Protestants. They were positive. They turned TO God. And observe, it *is* God. Not simply 'Jesus'. For, stealing his name *to make an idol out of their inventions*, calling the result 'Jesus', the modern evangelicals profess to have turned, that is, to be 'committed' to this 'Jesus'. But it is a Jesus of their own devising. And then their false Jesus so fills their mouths, and all their conversation, that one would not—from them—so much as know whether there be any *God*, as opposed to this idol 'Jesus' of theirs. But the true Christ is the mediator who *brings us to God*. Then these pretenders' 'Jesus' is false, who leaves us with himself: Here is ANOTHER JESUS. But the true Saviour brings us to, and reveals to us, HIS GOD AND FATHER by one Spirit. Hence 'Ye turned *to* God from idols.'

Hence conversion is not to the Son as such, but by him to *God in three Persons*, with all that this entails, and all that follows from it. And not to the—falsely so-called—theological, or merely doctrinal knowledge, or objective description, of God: BUT TO GOD HIMSELF, so as to *know him experimentally*. 'For this is life eternal, that they might know thee, the only true God, and Jesus Christ, whom thou hast sent.' Know him, that is, not by studying, not by listening to others, not by reading, not by professing, BUT BY TURNING:

1st., TO THE FATHER. So as to know him in a mystery, and to know his work by spiritual experience.

2nd., TO THE SON. So as to know his Person by union, and to know his work by the revelation of the gospel.

3rd., TO THE SPIRIT. So as to know him by the inward witness, and to know his work by interior power.

All this follows from a vital interest in and communion with God in three Persons. To this, *to God*, they turned, who were turned, at the beginning. Neither is there any other turning acknowledged in holy writ; this only is rock: all else is sand. All else is falsehood: shallow, vain, and empty pretence, by the which all who profess it will go to the judgment with a lie in their right hand, and a 'Lord, lord' in their empty mouths, to receive their just sentence from him whom they professed to know, but who will profess never to have known them, in that day, world without end.

As to the truly converted, they turned to the GOSPEL. Not to the LAW. FROM the law. Not to a mixture of law and gospel, that is, to a legal righteousness supposed to have been wrought out by Christ through an unlawful scheme of works of super-erogation. This mixture overturns the foundations, changing justifying righteousness from the righteousness of God by faith of Jesus Christ (Rom. 3:22) into the false and illegal notion of proxy law-keeping, supposed to produce vicarious legal works. All this is foisted upon Jesus Christ, profaning both him and the gospel. Not content therewith, afterwards this mixture goes on to RUIN THE LAW AS WELL AS THE GOSPEL, BESIDES THE BELIEVER, by putting those that are of faith back under the law as a rule of life, whilst robbing that law of its sanctions. Finally, to crown all their impertinence, the legalists call the apostles and Christ's ministers 'ANTINOMIAN'. FROM THIS THE EARLY, CONVERTED SAINTS TURNED, AND THEY TURNED TO THE PURITY OF THE APOSTOLIC GOSPEL, ALL OF WHICH, FROM FIRST TO LAST, WAS OF FAITH, 'from faith to faith, as it is written, The just shall live by faith.'*

*Read 'Deliverance from the Law: The Westminster Confession Exploded'. See Advertising Pages.

The early saints did not turn from idols by way of the second commandment of the law, in a way of works, which that commandment and law demanded, that by works they might turn to God. Turn to God by the commandment? Under the law God was beyond bounds, could not be approached, was hidden in thick darkness, behind the veil: how then could one turn to him? But in the gospel, APART FROM LAW, BOTH AS TO CHRIST'S BRINGING IN RIGHTEOUSNESS TO BE IMPUTED, AND IN OUR RECEIVING AND WALKING BY IT—'But now the righteousness of God WITHOUT THE LAW is manifested'—God gloriously reveals himself in the Son of his love, a free revelation gratuitously bestowed by grace: AND THIS TURNED THEM! It was the sight of Jesus Christ, and him crucified; the indwelling of the Holy Ghost; the partaking of the divine nature; and the Spirit of sonship freely poured out from the Father.

The early converts under the apostolic gospel turned to the company of God's people, *from* the carnal synagogue; they turned as pilgrims and strangers to the world to come, *from* the world that now is. They turned to an inward religion *from* the outward forms and the dead letter that left the interior parts untouched. They turned to 'all things become new': a new creation, a new Father, a new mother, new brethren, new sisters, new relationships, *from* all the old things, things of the flesh, of this present world, of the old man and the carnal birth, which shall surely pass away. *From* that, they turned.

Isa. 19, They turned unto the LORD. Neh. 1, They turned unto him, and kept his commandments. Psalm 119, They turned their feet unto HIS testimonies. Hos. 12, They answered the word, Turn unto thy God, and keep mercy and judgment. Mt. 18, They turned to become as little children. Acts 11,15 and 26, They turned to the LORD, Acts 26, to the LIGHT, Acts 26, to GOD. II Pet., They turned to the holy commandment delivered unto them, not *from* it. And in Acts 15, They turned to the brethren, and to the company of God's people.

Finally, as to THE WORK OF CONVERSION, this turning, under the head of being *radical*, is not only radical *in time*, not simply radical *in degree*, but it is also radical *in direction*.

Lastly, therefore, consider that this turning is radical in direction

Observe that it is a *radical* turn in direction. It is not a REFORMATION, it is a CONVERSION! It is described thus:

Deut. 30, If thou turn to the LORD thy God with all—mark that, ALL—thine heart. Observe, HEART. And Isa. chapter 6 clearly shows that a people must 'Understand with the HEART' to be converted. As says Joel, chapter 2, 'Rend your heart'— REND, notice; and, observe, the HEART—and so 'Turn unto the LORD.'

It is not a question of back to the BIBLE. It is not a matter of reforming your DOCTRINE. That is to rend *the garment*. But it is NOT RADICAL ENOUGH. Rend your HEART, saith Joel. It is not to begin to pray, meet with the people of God, take up the service of the Lord, go into the ministry, so-called: No. *All that is external to the heart.*

It is not a question of having gifts—Judas had gifts, of an order shared only by the other apostles. One may speak with the tongues of men and of angels, have the gift of prophecy, understand all mysteries, have all faith, possess all knowledge, but though internal to the flesh, all these things are external to the heart, and hence pertain to the garment, which is not to be rent, rather than to the heart, which is to be rent: CONVERSION IS A RADICAL TURNING OF THE HEART.

It is not a question of a change of motive. One's motive may change, and hence the fleshly bowels of Arminian compassion may flow, so that one bestows all one's goods to feed the poor. One's feelings may change, and from fervour in religion one may give one's body to be burned. One's affections may turn from the world to Jesus, and in consequence, out of the movings of universal charity, one may fall at his feet, weep over a lost world for very sentiment, cry 'Lord, Lord', and kiss him in the garden. But feelings, fiery zeal, warm emotion, flowing affections, natural sentiment, universal charity, all stand in the flesh, which is the garment, which, even if rent, falls vastly short of CONVERSION, being an abomination to the LORD in all its works, not requiring this at our hands, but only THE RENDING OF THE HEART.

Every one of these things may be done without a turning of the heart. They are no better than a change of opinion from one set of doctrines to another, however perfect the other may be. Indeed the doctrine to which men's minds turn may be perfect: but they are not: they draw nigh to him with their lips and head, but their heart is far from him, and the singleness God requires of the pure in heart—without which one shall not see God—IS A RADICAL TURNING OF THE RENT HEART. It is a 'Rend your *heart*' and nothing external to the heart. It is to 'obey from the heart' this very form of doctrine delivered in the gospel. Now, all things may be done in religion, so as—if it were possible—to deceive the very elect: for all these things may be done without a change of heart, however ardently they are done. BUT TRUE CONVERSION REACHES THE HEART, AND IT IS THERE THAT THE RADICAL TURNING TAKES PLACE. It is a radical turning of the very heart itself, in the innermost part of the inward man.

A ship on a certain great circular course will, virtually, maintain that course over vast stretches of the ocean. The direction, the compass point aimed at, the course, is fixed. All the seamen, the crew, in the vessel, from the masthead to the bowels of the ship, even down to the very bilges, necessarily are carried forward by the compass direction in which the vessel is travelling. They can go no other way. The vessel itself determines the direction they take. Nevertheless, the deceptive fact is this: the crew travels up and down, round and about, hither and thither, *in all kinds of directions, many of which are quite at variance to the way in which the vessel itself actually bears them along.* For example, a seaman on an urgent task may run from stem to stern, even faster than the vessel is travelling forward, actually hasting precisely in the opposite direction to that in which the ship is travelling. No matter. It avails nothing. He is *actually moved by the vessel in another direction to that in which apparently he is travelling.*

Whichever way the crew turn, however the seamen move, wherever they run, even counter to the course of the ship, in fact the vessel carries all on board, from the masthead to the keel of the ship, I say, the vessel carries all on board in one direction only. Their outward actions, contrary and deceptive, ACTUALLY MAKE NO DIFFERENCE AT ALL TO THE ULTIMATE DIRECTION IN WHICH THEY ARE GOING.

So it is with the heart: the heart maintains one direction, carrying all with it, just as does the ship carrying all the crew, irrespective of the actual movements of the seamen. All are carried along on one course, despite moving about irrespective of that course. This answers to the deceptiveness of the outward actions, changes of feeling, reformations of doctrine, alterations of mind, repentance of behaviour, and all the motley crew of the flesh, and of the soul. They may 'convert', going in precisely the opposite direction, it seems, to that in which they went before, but the heart is unchanged. It is still on the old course, deceitful appearances notwithstanding. And God abominates the deceitful appearances, requiring nothing less than a total 180°, radical change of direction from the innermost heart and life. This he calls CONVERSION. Anything less he rejects, and calls deception. 'For he is not a Jew, which is one outwardly: neither is that circumcision which is outward in the flesh: But he is a Jew, which is one inwardly; and circumcision is that of the heart, in the spirit, and not in the letter: whose praise is not of men, but of God.' JUST SO WITH SOUND CONVERSION.

The unregenerate, unquickened heart will remain in the old course of self-interest and self-gratification, but the means of self-interest, the mode of self-gratification may radically change, for example to religion, deceiving not only everybody else, but the blind, deluded soul itself. Still bound in the course of nature, utterly selfish and unchanged in heart, the outward man may convert to evangelical behaviour, a profession of Christ, a devotion to Jesus, or a so-called 'call' to the 'ministry'. Thus the heart interior, the ultimate unchanged direction of course, may be contradicted by the appearance of what is assumed to be a sound conversion. *But it is not.* The heart was never rent. The ultimate course was never changed. All that was converted was the fleshly, outward activity, the outward appearance, to another, a more religious, kind.

There may appear the most earnest bible reading, prayer, devotion, study, meetings, alms, religious duties, sacrifices, reaching to the giving of all one's goods, even to one's very life, say, in devout 'missionary' service, *but the old, self-centred, self-indulged, self-interested course still holds good: it is unchanged.* The members seem to run contrary to the old course; yes, but the vessel carries them on notwithstanding. The course remains unaltered. It is simply that a great deal of the activity, and the most visible of the activity, of the members on and within the vessel becomes outwardly religious, giving a contrary impression to those who look no further than the outward appearance. But the Lord does not look on the outward appearance. 'For the LORD looketh not on the outward appearance: the LORD looketh upon the heart.'

By appearance the members on board the vessel may at a time—if they were to be regarded—give the impression that the ship is travelling due East. For, at a command, at any one time, as it occurs, all crew members above and below decks may be ordered to walk towards the stern, that is, to the East. BUT THAT CHANGES NOTHING AS TO THE VESSEL ON WHOSE DECKS THEY WALK. *The vessel is still on its unchanged westerly*

course, whatever they do who are carried along by it. So IS
THE HEART TO THE OUTWARD APPEARANCE, AND TO THE MEMBERS.
*Conversion is a change of course, not of the members, but of the
vessel itself*: THE HEART. This carries all with it, but is itself
carried of none. There must be a radical change, a total change,
of the very course itself.

The whole vessel must swing right round. The entire ship
must revolve upon the ocean, IT revolves, carrying all with it,
it revolves through 180°, the vessel ITSELF carrying all as it
turns RADICALLY AND UTTERLY. The wake behind shows a vast
froth, a creamy swathe cut on the ocean, a vast 'U' turn is
painted enormously on the canvas of the sea: *there is no doubt
about that!* The course is altered 180°. The heart is rent, it is
turned radically, its direction is *utterly opposite*. It has *turned
180° in its ultimate direction*. So the heart, and the very life
within it, ALTER DIRECTION UTTERLY, RADICALLY: TO GOD from
selfishness, in the deepest intention of the being, and out of
the inmost well-springs of the life.

Now, in THE WORK OF CONVERSION, having seen that this
work is radical, and seen that it is radical in time; radical in
degree; and radical in direction; we come next to observe,

(ii) It is effectual

Because it springs from the quickening life of God, in which
the inner man has been born of God, born from above, born
of the Father and the Son, it is not subject to the vicissitudes,
vagaries, and changes that take place in the life of man. Man's
life has no stability, it turns every which way, and it is carried
about of winds, by fashions and trends, ever altering as the
years pass.

The natural man, with his changeable will, is constantly
subject to, nay, always looking for, change; that is, advant-
ageous change; change from contemporary pressures and
opportunities, from relationships of all kinds, and from circum-
stantial alterations made to gain advantage or avoid trouble.

There is no stable, settled principle, rooted in the natural life, much less from any turning, any supposed conversion, springing from that life; no, all is negotiable, and self-interest, whether in religion or not, makes for a constantly altering, changeable pattern.

Why? Because it is not rooted in everlasting life, which by definition and of necessity cannot change. There is no stay, no standing, nothing fixed in the religion of the natural man: his 'conversion' is nothing worth, because other things come in and take his desire: then, all adjusts accordingly. Money, fleshly relations, health, marriage, pleasure, prosperity, children, poverty, trials, afflictions, property, gain, security: all these change the natural man throughout his life. Hence he is continually ducking and weaving, always mutable, ever shifting for fleshly advantage, and to this, his evangelical profession of conversion, because it neither springs from the heart, nor the quickening of everlasting life, makes absolutely no difference at all: it simply changes with him, according to advantage. But true conversion, springing out of everlasting life, effectually fixes the soul. It keeps one; it preserves one in stability. The righteous shall not be moved. Their heart is fixed. They are like a tree planted by the rivers of waters which shall not be moved. Their principles are *utterly fixed*, springing from eternal life, which has once rent and effectively turned their heart for ever.

Again, true conversion is effectual, because it is not a matter of youthful enthusiasm. So much lies in this delusion today, in false and fickle evangelicalism. What an emphasis there is on youth! This is of necessity in such a system. Youthful enthusiasm, coupled with the ease with which youth may be manipulated by the unscrupulous, soon makes a fair show in the flesh, presenting a ready substitute for real conversion. Thus the puppeteers who pull the strings, the false physicians who tap the knee with the rubber hammer of their pop-gospel, easily gain a name in religion, they can pretend that something wonderful is happening: God is at work! *But he is not!*

It is just the natural reaction, the reflex, of youthful enthusiasm to the tricks of these devilish conjurors. And that is NOT THE TURNING, NOR IS IT THE CONVERSION, TRUE OF A RENT HEART.

It may seem like conversion to the superficial, but even to them, all becomes evident as youth dries up and age advances. But now the deceivers' attention is set on beguiling the next generation of the young: the ageing generation of yesterday's youth is quickly forgotten, and thus the practice of deceit, generated by the Deceiver, is perpetuated. But whoso is wise, and will observe these things, comparing them with a sound conversion, even they shall understand the lovingkindness of the LORD. For they wait on the LORD, and observe the effects of time. And it is soon apparent in the supposed 'conversion' of youthful enthusiasm, endorsed by deceivers that lightly heal the wound, and daub the outward wall with untempered mortar, that time has wilted the freshness of adolescence, so that the branch falls away to wither and die at the last.

But that can never happen with EVERLASTING LIFE, nor with what springs from it, namely, TRUE CONVERSION. That is as STABLE as it is EFFECTUAL. But youthful enthusiasm changes with time, dries up with age, becomes diverted by the desire of the eyes, by fleshly relationships, by covetousness, by ambition, by the fear of man, by advantage-seeking, and thus wanes. Then the young man or woman becomes indifferent to what before fired the enthusiasm, and sparked off the 'conversion', so-called, because the soul becomes taken up with the deceitfulness of riches, the lust of the eye, the lust of the flesh, the pride of life, the affairs of this life, with house, family, husband, wife, children, job, and so *all dries up from the root, that had seemed so lively at the start.* Soon, spurious youthful conversions, called for by deceivers who use and abuse the young for effect, that is, to pretend to being fruitful, sacrificing youth on the altar of their own self-importance, soon, I say, 'conversion', sprung up from fleshly zeal, dries up. BUT GOD SHALL BRING ALL INTO JUDGMENT.

However, real conversion, having its root in everlasting life, cannot change. It is effectual because *nothing can alter eternal life*. It is divinely stable.

True conversion is not that which comes from fearful, or lonely, old age. Here, longing for companionship, or the dread of being left alone, or, worse still, the imminence of death at the last, frightens the aged, and starts up the old religion again, just before the soul hurtles into eternity. Not so true conversion. In true conversion, fruit is borne in old age, like the tree planted by the rivers of waters, the leaf never fades, fruit, brought forth in every season, hangs thick on the gnarled old boughs, the roots drawing strength and moisture out of the river of God, preserving not the seed of nature, but the planting of the Father, and hence effectual *throughout the life* to the very end. Because a true work springs not from natural life, but from the life of God himself, the Eternal, upon whose divine life both time and its decaying work are utterly ineffectual, totally impotent. THIS IS CONVERSION.

It is effectual, *because such a turning ensures lifelong direction and lifelong perseverance.* This is revealed by the life, by the heart, and by the continuous conversation. United to the Son of God within, from the womb of the morning this divine seed has the dew of its youth even unto old age: its youth is *renewed* like the eagle's. The conversion flows fresh again and again continually in living streams.

Hence it is that the converted turn from their old conversation, and, ever refreshed, again and again, consistently maintain the new conversation. This is indicated by the same verb, or stem, STREPHŌ, but with a different prefix or preposition, ANA, where ANASTREPHŌ gives the meaning 'turn again', as opposed to EPISTREPHŌ, 'turn upon'. ANASTREPHŌ is to turn again and again, turn consistently, so as to maintain not the old, but an entirely new, renewed, conversation.

Eph. 4, Put off the old *conversation*. Jas. 3, Show a good *conversation*. Heb. 13, Remember them that have the rule over you, who have spoken unto you the word of God: whose faith follow, considering the *end* of their *conversation*. II Pet. 3, In the fear of God show all holy *conversation*. I Pet. 1, Be ye holy in all manner of *conversation*, I Pet. 2, Having your *conversation* honest among the Gentiles.

This is the consequence of a sound conversion, not just turning at one given moment, not just once in a while, not merely as a youth, but as a *perpetual course*, as a matter of *conversation*. And what a change of course! I Pet. 3, Wives, women, being marked by *chaste conversation*, coupled with fear—the opposite to the old worldly fashion, dress, cosmetics —adorning (*kosmetikos*) the hair, putting on of apparel— eschewing jewellery, ornaments, rings of all sorts: whether put on in the apostate 'churches' or not! Christ and the apostles, the bible and the new testament scriptures, forbad any such superstitious, pagan, and worldly practices, all forms of 'luck', 'charms', cosmetics, and feminine worldliness being roundly denounced by the apostles Peter and Paul. For in contrast to such things the apostles commended the sole ornament of *the hidden man of the heart*, in meekness and true subjection. Then the household, and others, are won, I Pet. 3:1, without the word, by this interior, chaste conversation. That is, conversation marked by a steady, consistent course.

How different from the apostasy, the sects, the denominations, from fallen evangelicalism, from the charismatic pretence, from Protestant fundamentalism, with all its humbug, especially in the lawless uprising of their women against Christ, against the order of God, and against the headship of the man! *But never so in the converted!* Only so in the unconverted. The converted are converted *from that*. How different their TURNING! How effectual their CONVERSATION! Because of a SOUND CONVERSION. This springs up from the vital quickening of life, and is preceded by the sound preparation of the alarm, the awakening, the conviction, leading to that mighty quickening, that springing well, those flowing waters, the living streams, so that the TURNING, the CONVERSION, issues from the life of God in the heart, welling up through the whole soul, out through every faculty and attribute, pouring out through the conversation, to yield over the years of a consistent lifetime, *a sound, good, effectual conversation.* This is the true witness of the grace of God that brings salvation, leading in the process of the work of God by the Spirit to Saving Faith in Christ, to the glory and praise of God.

REPENTANCE

VI

Repentance

6. REPENTANCE

(i) The importance of repentance

JOHN the baptist preached it. Therefore it heralded, and spiritually still heralds, the coming of Christ. John cried, saying, Mt. 3:2, 'Repent ye: for the kingdom of heaven is at hand.' Nor can time change the message or the messenger. He, being dead, yet speaketh. It is historically true that Christ was made manifest to the Jews, Acts 13:24, 'When John had first preached before his coming the baptism of repentance to all the people of Israel.' And it is just as true that it is as spiritually necessary in the history of the soul now, as it was in the history of Israel then.

Jesus preached it. Therefore it characterised the preaching of Christ. Mt. 4:17, 'From that time Jesus began to preach, and to say, Repent: for the kingdom of heaven is at hand.' And the repentance Jesus preached, evidently preceded not only the kingdom, but saving faith, for he saith, Mk. 1:15, 'The time is fulfilled, and the kingdom of God is at hand: repent ye, and believe the gospel.'

Repentance saved vast cities of old time. Lk. 11:32, 'The men of Nineveh ... repented at the preaching of Jonas.' Yet, 'Behold, a greater than Jonas is here.' Then even greater repentance is called for in our day, and more conspicuous, than was theirs in that day.

77

The apostles preached repentance. The *ecclesia* built by Christ is founded upon the apostolic preaching of the doctrine of the gospel being inwardly and spiritually applied, resulting in adult penitents, forthwith baptized, being gathered together in one under the apostles' doctrine and fellowship, the breaking of bread, and prayers. Acts 2:38, 'Then Peter said unto them, Repent, and be baptized every one of you in the name of Jesus Christ for the remission of sins, and ye shall receive the gift of the Holy Ghost.' And again, Acts 17:30, 'God commandeth all men everywhere to repent.' Acts 20:21, 'Preaching repentance toward God, and faith toward our Lord Jesus Christ.'

No other religious exercise, spiritual experience, heavenly vision, divine ecstasy, supernatural gift, or mystical operation is a substitute for, or will be counted in lieu of, or shall ever stand as surety in the place appointed for repentance in the counsels of God. Repentance is a *sine qua non*. It is indispensable, and in that order in which it appears, and is called forth, by the work of God leading to saving faith.

Hence, there is no substitute for repentance in the work of salvation. Lk. 16:29,30, Abraham replied unto the departed, tormented, soul, 'They have Moses and the prophets; let them hear them'—that is, let the tormented man's brothers, still alive on earth in this world, hear them—'And he', the dead, tormented man, his soul in the flames, who asked to visit his living brethren, deceived in this world, to warn them, 'he said, Nay, father Abraham: but if one went' unto them 'from the dead, they will REPENT.' But Abraham said unto him, 'If they hear not Moses and the prophets, neither will they be persuaded, though one rose from the dead.'

The importance of repentance is seen further by the coming of Christ into the world. Mt. 9:13, Jesus said, 'I am not come to call the righteous, but sinners to repentance'; So also Mk. 2:17. Again, Lk. 24:47, Jesus, risen from the dead, appeared and stood in the midst of the apostles, showing them his hands

78

and his feet, and saying, 'A spirit hath not flesh and bones as ye see me have'. He ate fish and an honeycomb before them all. He opened by divine and interior power the inward understanding of each one of them, that they might understand the scriptures. Then he said, 'Preach REPENTANCE and remission of sins in my name, among all nations.' After this he ascended into heaven.

Once more, Acts 20:21, Paul testified both to the Jews and also to the Greeks, 'REPENTANCE TOWARD GOD, and faith toward our Lord Jesus Christ.' Where the one is not only stressed as much as the other, but REPENTANCE COMES FIRST. And this is evident, for, Lk. 13:3,5, 'Except ye repent, ye shall all likewise perish.'

(ii) The meaning of repentance

That is, the meaning of the word 'repentance'. It must be admitted straight away that this English word is totally inadequate to convey the force of the new testament Greek which it has been used to translate in the scriptures. Nor can I find or suggest any alternative in English that *is* adequate. The Greek simply does not *mean* what the English conveys. But first, what *does* the English mean, and from whence did the word arise?

The English word REPENT comes from the French *repentir*, meaning, 'repentance', 'contrition', 'regret', or, 'to repent', 'to rue'. This French word is derived in turn from the combination of the prefix *re* and the Romance word *penitire*. The latter in turn finds its source in the Latin *paenitere*, 'to be sorry', 'to regret', 'to repent'. Observe that, via the Romance and the French, this Latin word is at the root of the English 'REPENT', but it is not at the root of nor is it connected with the word used in the new testament Greek. The English 'repent' has a Latin root, and not a Greek root, even though many other English words are derived from the Greek language. In this case the source meaning of the English word

79

used to translate the Greek of the new testament *is from another language—French—and derived from a different root altogether, namely, the Latin.* With such a word, this matters greatly.

Hence the meaning of the English REPENT of course reflects the Latin root and the French branch: *'To feel contrition, compunction, sorrow or regret for something one has done or left undone: to change one's mind with regard to past action or conduct through dissatisfaction with it or its results. To be sad; to mourn. To view with dissatisfaction or regret, to feel contrition, to sorrow.'* But this, however faithful to the Latin, is not what the new testament Greek means: it is only the word foisted upon that Greek, to translate it into English. Now, therefore, consider the Greek of the scriptures, for here lies a fundamental difference. *The English word and the Latin source both look for a meaning in the* FEELINGS. *The Greek does not. Its meaning lies in the* MIND.

The word in the Greek new testament everywhere translated REPENT (thirty-four times) and REPENTANCE (twenty-four times) is a compound, respectively METANOEŌ, 'repent', and META-NOIA, 'repentance'. In fact, there *is* a Latin equivalent to this word, more or less, but it is *not* the Latin word which is the root of the English 'repentance'. Another Latin word altogether, it is *RESIPISCO* 'to recover one's senses', 'to come to a right understanding'. As opposed to *feelings*, here is a word indicative of a *change of mind*. Quite unlike the English 'repentance', and its Latin source *paenitere*, the Latin *resipisco* answers to the Greek METANOIA, having to do entirely with the *mentality*, and not at all pointing to the sensibility.

The compound METANOEŌ, 'repent'—the verb—or META-NOIA, 'repentance'—the noun form—is derived from the prefix META, and the stem NOIA, or, of course, the stem NOEŌ in the case of the verb form.

First, the prefix META. This preposition bears the general meaning of 'in the midst of, between, in common with'. If used—with the accusative—of sequence or succession, it may mean 'after, behind (as sheep which follow after the leader); beyond, far side'. Again, in terms of time, this flexible preposition will refer to 'after, next to, thereupon, next after'. The idea in common remains 'between'; 'in the midst', but the bewildering variety of applications make the word difficult to grasp with precision.

In connection with METANOIA, META has the significance of *the change that lies in time*, between *what went before, and what comes after*. In this case META, basically 'between, in the midst', should be translated as indicating *after the passing of time*, 'thereafter, next after'. Or to be as precise as possible with this compound, 'afterwards': *first* this; *then* that.

The stem, or main, word in the compound is NOIA, or, of course, NOEŌ. This is the word used for 'mind'. The North-country colloquialism 'nous' actually transliterates this Greek word. Although 'mind' is the usual translation, this implies a limitation to one area of the mental faculties, but there is no doubt that a broader, and far superior, translation would be 'MENTALITY'. Mentality takes in the mind, but it takes in other, indeed all, mental faculties besides—which is in itself better—and, best of all, *it indicates the state of those faculties as a whole*: THE MENTALITY.

One cannot do better than that. But what is the force upon this of the prefix META?

METANOIA, or METANOEŌ, presses home the preposition META in terms of *the mentality*. How? Used as a prefix in the compound it indicates *a point of focus in time upon the state of the mentality* BEFORE *which one condition obtained, and* AFTER *which another condition prevailed*. A change occurred in the mentality in the midst of its existence in time *before* which it was one thing, and *after* which it was another. It indicates something in respect of the mentality *sufficiently drastic to say*,

'that, yes; but before'; now, 'afterwards', something has occurred to the mentality which necessitates our saying, 'between
these two periods'; 'in the midst' of these really distinct states,
THE MENTALITY CHANGED.

The sum is this: the Greek indicates the entire inwardness
of the mind, rather, the whole mentality, to which is applied
a contrast, a change, in the passage of time, as, beforehand,
then, afterwards. Thus, crudely, in the most limited sense,
'afterthought, after mind', and so, 'to change the mind'. That
is, AFTERWARDS TO HAVE ANOTHER MENTALITY THAN THAT WHICH
WENT BEFORE. 'A change of mind or mentality.' This occurs
some sixty times in the new testament.

Since the faculty referred to as *afterwards*, or *following after*,
being distinct from *what it was before*, is the whole *mentality*,
then, METANOIA cannot just be a change of feelings. Although the English 'repent' implies this, the Greek does not,
in fact the Greek makes no reference to the feelings. However
deep or affected the feelings which precede, accompany, or
follow *this change of mentality*, the word METANOIA has in
itself no reference to them whatsoever, because, whatever else
happens, it happens as a result of *the change that takes place in
the mentality*, and nothing and nowhere else.

METANOIA does not indicate a change of heart. That is,
unless the very broad use of the word heart in the scripture
should be used loosely in any one given place to mean the
inward mentality. But the heart as the seat of the sensibility,
whether the affections, the passions, the emotions; or the heart
as the seat of the will, whether the intentions, the resolutions,
or that voluntary rule governing the course of the life: no;
METANOIA does not refer to any of these things, however
they may be affected in consequence of the change of mentality. The point is, *it is the change of mentality that changes them.*
Their change is not at all indicated by the word METANOIA.
The change of *mentality* alone is indicated by the word
METANOIA. Otherwise the word would be METAKARDIA,

change of heart, but it is not, it is METANOIA, *change of mentality.* THAT makes the change. THAT is the seat of the change. THAT changes all else. Every other change is indirect, resulting from the changed mentality. *There* is the seat of the change.

METANOIA is not indicative in itself of a change of conduct. No doubt the conduct is changed, indeed, transformed, *but that is not the object of METANOIA, it is the effect of it.* Whatever the effect on the conduct or the behaviour, *it is the mentality that is changed, and that alone,* all the rest is the *effect* of THAT change. Then, 'repentance' or penitence, is certainly not an outward reformation, or even a forsaking of sin, or the world, in and of itself considered. *It is to change one's whole mind, to have the entire mentality altered or transformed.* All these other things take the place of being an *effect,* from the cause of METANOIA. THAT is the real change, and THAT is what gives rise to any external reformation, or forsaking of sin, or departing from the world. The one is the INTERIOR CAUSE the other the OUTWARD EFFECT.

(iii) The reason for repentance

This is to be found in the previous state of mind. The prior mental condition of humanity. The universal mentality of mankind, considered in its essence, reveals the cause of God's commanding all men everywhere to repent. What is this state of mind?

Firstly, It is naturally reprobate. Rom. 1:28, 'God gave them over to a reprobate mind.' II Tim. 3:8, 'Minds reprobate concerning the truth.'

Secondly, It is naturally corrupt. I Tim. 6:5, 'Men of corrupt minds.' Titus 1:15, 'Even their mind and conscience is defiled.'

Thirdly, It is naturally vain. Eph. 4:17, 'The nations walk in the vanity of their minds', being, Col. 2:18, 'Vainly puffed up in their fleshly minds.'

Fourthly, It is naturally alien. Col. 1:21, 'Ye were enemies to God in your minds.' Rom. 8:7, 'The carnal mind is enmity against God.'

Fifthly, It is naturally darkened. II Cor. 4:4, 'The god of this world hath blinded the minds of them which believe not', Eph. 4:18, 'Having the understanding darkened', because, II Cor. 3:14, 'Their minds were blinded.'

These are the reasons that men ought to repent. Because as to God, as to the law, as to judgment, as to accountability, as to the wrath to come, as to the resurrection, as to eternity, as to the Fall, as to the brevity of life, as to the vanity of this world, as to immortality, the mind of all mankind is dark as the pit, blind as a bat, being utterly void of the sight of reality. The entire mental processes of all mankind, throughout, from the inner consciousness, through reason, intellect, understanding, are in a state of darkness, blind and deluded.

Neither can any outward means, law, commandments, morality, philosophy, scriptures, nor yet Christ himself outwardly conceived, or historically known, or sentimentally imagined, nor the bible, the church, services, confessions, professions, memberships, descriptions of or calls from men to come to Jesus, make the slightest difference to this inward blindness and interior darkness of the mind. The law may describe what is holy and just and good; the gospel may describe a Christ and his work of salvation; but all such descriptions are given to men blind, dark, and unable to conceive of such things within themselves. They cannot see the things described. They cannot make out the reality of that which is set forth. How can they? They are without sight in the dark. It is *this* that requires repentance: it is *a new mentality*, one that is *illuminated*, to which *sight has been given*, that is needed. Such a change, METANOIA describes.

Though commanded, for it ought to be rendered, and the true state admitted, and repented of, and a new mentality produced by the preaching of the glorious gospel of Christ, nevertheless, it is in God's gift. 'God', Acts 5:31, *'gives* repentance to Israel.' 'God hath', Acts 11:18, *'granted* repentance unto the Gentiles.' That men *ought* to repent, but aggravates their obdurate impenitence, for none do, no, not one, such is the blind obstinacy of man. Even though there be some negative awareness of the inner darkness of the mind, still, none repent unless the gift of God grant that to which the natural mentality is utterly and churlishly opposed.

But what of the law? Will that not penetrate the mind, and bring about repentance, although the gospel has not yet penetrated the mentality? It will not. If true repentance once appear, then it is certain, it is *despite* the law not because of it. Legal repentance is a fiction. True repentance is *because of the gospel*, and because of the goodness of God commanding the light thereof, in the face of Jesus Christ, to shine into the otherwise blind and darkened heart. 'Knowest thou not that *the goodness of God leadeth thee'*—mark that, *leadeth* thee—'to repentance?' Rom. 2:4. Then, it is the peradventure of God, not the legal rule, not the latent glimmer in the reason of man, that brings repentance worth the name, by the gift of grace. 'If peradventure God will *give* them repentance to the acknowledging of the truth', II Tim. 2:25.

(iv) The cause of repentance

The cause is not, and cannot be, the outward law or the carnal commandments, even if received spiritually. 'The law worketh wrath', and nothing else. Indeed, 'When the commandment came'—spiritually—saith Paul, 'sin revived, and I died.' And that is all the ministration of the law can do: sentence to death. But has a dead man a change of mentality? Then how can the law bring repentance? The truth is that the law can never at any time, or in any way, alone; by itself; mixed with the gospel; confused with faith; the law, I say, can never at any time, or in any way, be anything other than a ministration of death. It can never bring anything but a killing sentence, it can never be anything but the dead letter. The law will, for it must, sound out a continual curse, called down on all under it, who, without exception, have failed of its demands to 'do this and live'. Thus, fallen, stumbling over every conditional promise, being laid under bands and chains, and an iron yoke, such bondslaves to sin must await that certain, fearful, and looked-for judgment, until and unless brought to evangelical repentance by the light of the gospel.

The cause of repentance lies exclusively, not in a legal or moral reformation to the law or the commandments, but in the glorious gospel of Christ. And at that, such being the blind and darkened state of mankind, only when God gives interior sight, and inward illumination, when, 'the light of the glorious gospel shines in unto them', when 'God, who commanded the light to shine out of darkness, hath shined in our hearts, to give the light of the knowledge of the glory of God in the face of Jesus Christ.' That changes the mentality. And *that change of mentality*, called METANOIA, is what is meant by the new testament Greek rendered by the English word 'repentance' in the bible.

Hence *revelation* is the spring of repentance: it is by this issue and precedent. Although men *ought* to render penitence, they *will* not, because they love darkness rather than light. But did they not—in their rebellion refusing the commandment of God—did they not love darkness rather than light, such a revelation of the gospel of Christ still remains God's gift, granting repentance by the gift of sight, and the inshining of revelation. Hence it is 'Be ye transformed by the renewing of your minds', Rom. 12:2; 'Being renewed in the *spirit* of your minds', Eph. 4:23; that is, Eph. 1:18, when 'the eyes of your *understanding* are'—not instructed; not educated; but—'*enlightened*'. This takes place when, Lk. 24:45, Christ *opens*—*He* opens—up their understanding. Thus God *puts* his laws—that is, the law of faith; the law of liberty;

the law of Christ; the law of the Spirit of life—he *puts* his laws into the heart, and he *writes* them in the mind. And, since all stands in the Father's revealing the Son, it follows that 'The Son of God hath given us an understanding', I Jn. 5:20.

This illumination, this inward revelation, gives light, opens blind eyes, rends the veil between the soul and God, dispenses with human priesthood and an earthly temple, shines directly from the Father, immediately reveals the Son, discloses him within, stands in the Person, presence, power and indwelling of the Holy Ghost, radiates and pulsates through the word of truth, the gospel of our salvation, and shines out through the doctrine of Christ. This CHANGES THE MENTALITY in a moment; consistently; permanently; and ever-increasingly, for the path of the just is as a shining light, that shineth more and more unto the perfect day. All who are in the secret are changed from glory to glory, even as by the Spirit of the Lord. They go from strength to strength every one of them in Zion appearing before God. This is the generation of them that seek him, that seek thy face, O Jacob. Selah.

(v) The effect of repentance

The declaration of remission of sins always accompanies evangelical—the only true—repentance. The penitent immediately, invariably, always and wholly has his sins forgiven. Without it, therefore, he does not. Observe: Mk. 1:4, 'Preach the baptism of repentance for the remission of sins.' Lk. 3:3, 'Preaching the baptism of repentance for the remission of sins.' Lk. 24:47, Jesus commanded the apostles 'That repentance and remission of sins should be preached in his name among all nations, beginning at Jerusalem.' Acts 5:31, 'Jesus hath God exalted with his right hand to be a Prince and a Saviour, for to give repentance to Israel, and forgiveness of sins.'

Believing the gospel always follows on with repentance. It is 'repentance toward God', not in respect of the law, or of

Moses, or the ten commandments, but in respect of 'faith toward our Lord Jesus Christ', Acts 20:21. It is to repent toward God, not because Moses gave the law, but because the Father sent the Son. 'For the law was given by Moses', and brought in not one penitent, but brought down wrath and a curse, bringing to light the incorrigible nature of man's lawlessness in the Fall, 'For by the law is the knowledge of sin'. 'But grace and truth came by Jesus Christ', and from this came the call for evangelical repentance for the remission of sins through faith in his name.

Repentance therefore is to have another mind about the *gospel*! Not the *law*! It is to have a change of mentality because the Father sent the *Son*. Not sent the *commandments*! It is to have another mentality on account of the truth that God was in Christ reconciling the world unto himself; that God gave him as a propitiation for the whole world; that he is the Lamb of God that taketh away the sin of the world; that God so loved the world that he gave his only begotten Son; that the Father sent the Son to be the Saviour of the world. That is what calls for a new mentality, a change of mind, by that mind, that mentality, being filled with the light of the glorious gospel, with the truth of the Father and the Son, with the doctrine of justification, propitiation, remission, reconciliation, ransom, atonement, substitution, redemption, and every harmonious truth which united together in one constitutes *the* truth, the sum of which shining in the mind gives ANOTHER MENTALITY to every true penitent.

Whereas the clergy, the traditions of the elders, and the rotten theologies and confessions which men have invented, lisped out by all the confused hirelings in the pulpits, join repentance to Moses, the law, and the commandments, which never did anything but slay, kill, curse, and shut up to darkness and wrath. Such are unable to bring forth one act of righteousness, one gasp of penitence, or one breath of repentance. For the law was delivered thousands and thousands of years—achieving nothing but the exposure of sin, the sounding of the curse, and the sentence of death—thousands of years before the Father sent the Son, before the promised gospel came into the world, before the first apostolic herald sounded 'REPENT YE, AND BELIEVE THE GOSPEL', and before evangelical repentance, the only thing that ever turned men from darkness to light, from evil to good, from iniquity to righteousness, I say, before evangelical repentance began its course to run with the gospel throughout the world to the end of the age.

Being baptized also accompanies repentance, where baptism, a new testament ordinance, is joined with evangelical penitence, *a change of mentality, another mind, about the gospel* so as to fill the mentality, to transform it, with evangelical truth. And, hence, to be baptized is to set this forth in a figure: Acts 2:38, 'Repent, and be baptized every one of you.' Mk. 1:4, The beginning of the gospel of Jesus Christ, the Son of God: John preached in the wilderness 'the baptism of repentance for the remission of sins.' Acts 13:24, 'this baptism of repentance is to all the people of Israel', and, Acts 19:4, 'the disciples were baptized with the baptism of repentance.'

Oh, what a change of mentality! What a power of the Holy Ghost to accomplish repentance! If so, then what a change is called for from the presumptuously religious, from those resting in false claims, in systems which can never save, from a mentality binding together Christ and Moses, justification and legal obedience, remission of sins and the ten commandments, and from the law—which Paul found to be death—being counted as the believer's rule of life! What kind of mentality holds this? One that needs A THOROUGH CHANGE! Should not this make such ministers, pastors, and clergy, to tremble?

'O generation of vipers, who hath warned you to flee from the wrath to come? Bring forth therefore fruits meet for repentance' by no longer building here three tabernacles, one for

Moses, one for Elias, and—by the way—one for Jesus. THEIR
MENTALITY IS CLOUDED. But if God break through, dispelling
the darkness of their minds, they shall see no man, save Jesus
only, and hear nothing—much less Moses or the voice of angels
on Sinai's mount upon earth thousands of years ago—nothing
but the present voice of the Father from heaven, answering
to the divine vision of his Son, and saying from the excellent
glory: '*This is my beloved Son: hear him.*' And no one else, much
less Moses or Elias. Besides hearing no speech or doctrine other
than that of the gospel of the grace of Christ, quite removed
and apart from the condemnation of the law of Moses.

(vi) The necessity of repentance

It is necessary because of the heinous wickedness of impenitence and unbelief. Consider the dreadful condition of mankind,
of a world, knowing that the Father sent the Son, knowing
that there is a gospel of the grace of Christ, the gospel of God
concerning his Son, and yet remaining indifferent, apathetic,
and, worse, wilfully impenitent despite it. Here is a generation
flagrantly unrepentant. It is not that they do not know. They
know, the apostate worldly 'church' knows, the world knows,
but what it knows it tramples underfoot as the mire of the
streets. They WILL NOT. The world, and the worldly 'church',
wickedly refuses to repent. The whole world, and the whole
of worldly religion, lies in this common wickedness, forgetting
the truth of the gospel if possible, perverting it if not, meanwhile occupying one another in a vain round of frivolous
diversion, chaffy conversation, airy notion, worldly entertainment, carnal pleasure, and foolish behaviour, PRETENDING
THAT ALL IS WELL.

But all is NOT WELL. Soon the music will stop. The image will
flicker, fade, and die out. The earth and the inhabitants
thereof will be turned upside down. The heavens shall roll
together as a scroll, and all the host of them shall fall. Then it

shall not be well. Then it shall go ill with all the impenitent. Hence, Acts 2:38, it is 'Repent and be baptized *every one*', yes, and even more direct, 'every one *of you*.' And again, Acts 17:30, 'God commandeth *all men*'—and as if that were not pointed enough—'all men *everywhere*' to repent. Once more, you are admonished and solemnly warned that, Acts 26:20, 'Ye should repent and turn to God', and, moreover, from faith and love in Christ by the Holy Ghost in the gospel, '*do works meet for repentance*', that is, show forth the transformation of your mentality by behaviour becoming the truth of Christ.

Now, therefore, being forewarned of the judgment of God, we are not to slight the command of the most High, for, II Pet. 3:9, 'He is not willing that any should perish, but that all should come to repentance.' Beware of apathetic neglect of penitence, as of wilfully despising the command to repent, for there are those 'who, being often reproved, harden their neck.' These are without remedy, whom, Heb. 6:6, 'It is impossible to renew again unto repentance.' They are like Esau, who was of the seed of Abraham, born of Isaac; he was Jacob's brother, yet he sold his heavenly birthright for a mess of earthly pottage. Yet even he was shocked into reality by what he had done, who squandered both birthright and blessing. Hence, afterwards, 'He sought repentance carefully'—mark that, carefully—'with tears'—observe, with tears—'but', Heb. 12:17, 'HE FOUND NO PLACE FOR IT.' It was far too late, and he had gone far beyond the point of no return.

Let men think again, therefore, of this gospel. Let them ponder the end of their present mentality. For, refusing to repent, disobeying the gospel, slighting the Father, rejecting the Son, denying the Holy Ghost, one can never be more evil or more wicked in the sight of God. Those who do so are as wholly in a state of iniquity and of total disobedience as is the devil himself. Hence these goats, but none of Christ's sheep, shall share this sentence, 'Depart from me, ye cursed, into everlasting fire, prepared for the devil and his angels', Mt. 25:41.

Saving Faith

Let those who are pricked in their heart consider these things, and consider their latter end, and *repent and believe the gospel*. And bring forth fruits meet for such a repentance, such a total change of mentality as fills the mind with light where there had been darkness, with the doctrine of Christ where there had been self-centred and worldly thoughts, with the power of the Holy Ghost where before the delusions and lies of Satan had reigned. May the Lord grant repentance unto life, that many may '*repent, and be b ptized*', having that CHANGE OF MENTALITY which glorifies Christ, and magnifies his work, in the power of God, and the light of the glorious gospel of his Son.

FAITH

VII
Faith

7. Faith

I. What Faith is Not

(i) It is not of the law

PAUL declares, Gal. 3:12, 'The law is not of faith'. Then faith is not of the law. The law did not demand faith, and not one of its commandments required belief: all demanded works. Not only did no single command of the law require faith, the law as a whole had nothing to do with faith, neither faith with it. The old covenant, the law of Moses, the ten commandments, the entire legal system, never mentions or requires faith, and if the words faith, belief, or trust occur in the old testament, they occur only as they reflect the promise of a gospel yet to come, received in type, figure, shadow, and prophecy by those of old time, as it is said, 'And the scripture, foreseeing that God would justify the heathen through faith, preached before the gospel unto Abraham', Gal. 3:8. But what is that to do with the law? Indeed, the law was not in the world at all until some four hundred and thirty years after Abraham departed this scene to be gathered to his fathers.

The law knows nothing of faith, belief, or trust, it requires works on pain of death, it presupposes ability and demands obedience, 'The man that doeth them shall live in them'. The law is all of works, requiring perfect obedience for life on earth, and sentencing to death those who do not render it absolutely and continually: 'Cursed is every one that continueth not in all things written in the book of the law to do them.' Then, the law is not of faith, and knows nothing of belief. Such things come from another quarter, and belong to a better covenant, founded upon better promises. They are never, no, never mixed together.

And since faith is not of law, which demands works, it follows, neither is faith of works, nor is it to be confused or confounded in any way with the works of the law. The law requires works, nothing more nor less, and that fully as to capacity, profoundly as to depth, and continually as to time. There is no question of what one believes: it is irrelevant. There is no question as to mercy: that has nothing to do with the law. The law prescribes, defines, requires and commands that rule of righteousness obligatory upon man to perform, and it will have commensurate works, or curse the transgressor to death. 'Cursed is every one that continueth not in all things that are written in the book of the law to do them.' Do them. And do *all things* written in the book. And *continue* to do them. To all who come short of this, the curse is inexorable and final. Faith does not appear. 'For if they which are of the law be heirs, faith is made void', Rom. 4:14, 'and the promise made of none effect.'

Why is faith made void by the law? Why does the law make the promise of none effect? Because the law requires no faith, only works. And the promise is to faith, not works. The promise requires no works, only faith. And the promise came not by works, it came by hearing. 'Received ye the Spirit by the works of the law, *or* by the hearing of faith?' Gal. 3:2. Yea, Rom. 3:28, we are 'justified by faith *without* the deeds of the law.' And without the law itself, which requires legal deeds, knows no grace, and admits of no faith whatsoever. Why not? Because there is nothing to believe about the law.

Only to do. Whereas there is nothing to do about faith. Only to believe.

'For Moses', Rom. 10:5, 'describeth the righteousness which is of the law', saying, 'the man which DOETH those things shall live by them'; BUT the righteousness of faith speaketh on another wise, and declares, Rom. 10:4, 'Christ is the END of the law for righteousness to every one that believeth.' 'And if by grace, then is it no more of works: otherwise grace is no more grace', Rom. 11:6, 'But if it be of works, then it is no more grace: otherwise work is no more work.' Clearly then, FAITH IS NOT OF WORKS. Whereas the law sounds a curse, 'Cursed is every one'; faith gives a blessing, 'So then they which be of faith are blessed with faithful Abraham', Gal. 3:9. Moreover, 'by the law is the knowledge of sin', Rom. 3:20, 'but by faith is the remission of sins.' And again, 'The law worketh wrath', Rom. 4:15, but, Rom. 5:1, Justification by faith brings peace.

Furthermore, Abraham is the father of the faithful, Rom. 4:11, in that he, Gen. 15:6, 'Believed in the LORD, and he counted it to him for righteousness.' And this righteousness, or justification, by faith, or belief, of Abraham and all that seed of whom he is regarded as the father, the law, Gal. 3:17, which was four hundred and thirty years afterwards, cannot disannul, that it should make the promise of none effect. At the time at which Abraham was justified by faith alone, Gen. 15:6, Abraham was uncircumcised, had no knowledge of law, there was no law, he knew nothing whatsoever of its works, he walked by faith, he lived by faith, he obtained a good report by faith, he was justified by faith, he was heir to the righteousness of faith, he looked for a heavenly country by faith, he waited for a heavenly city by faith, he believed in the resurrection by faith, and he was promised the world to come by faith. And what assistance was the then non-existent law in all that, and what ever could the law possibly add, when it did come four hundred and thirty years later? What could the law add to all that grace had already given to faith, in an everlasting covenant eternally secure, confirmed by an immutable oath, and settled by an unbreakable promise?

By faith Abraham subdued kingdoms, turned to flight the armies of the aliens, wandered about as a sojourner on earth, believed in a better resurrection, overcame sin and death, raised up seed when past age, and at last, not having received the promises, still strong in faith, still giving glory to God, still not regarding corruption, decay, mortality or death, still staggering not at the promises of God through unbelief, at last I say, in triumph and glory, Abraham even died in faith! And he never knew the law, he never had any idea or dream of its works, and, had he, he would have shunned the whole legal system like the plague, since already he possessed all, and more than all, in an unconditional blessing freely given of God and sworn by an immutable oath. Now then what hast thou to do with the law? What hast thou to do to meddle with its works? Turn thee behind me, and follow the chariot to glory, crying, 'My father, my father, the chariot of Israel, and the horsemen thereof', for this alone, long before the law, carried Israel and his seed into heaven, world without end, Amen.

(ii) It is not in isolation

Faith has precedents, it has origins, faith has consequences, it is not isolated, it is not as if it were a thing in and of itself, subsisting alone in its own character and nature: it is part of a whole, not a whole in itself. Faith does not simply arrive unheralded, it is preceded by an alarm, the sinner is awakened, the wrath of God is revealed, conviction of sin follows, the poor soul cries out to God, he is quickened, he is turned, in the power of that life he is converted, he repents towards God, *thus he comes to saving faith*: out of that regenerating life HE BELIEVES ON THE LORD JESUS CHRIST; Oh, yes, there are precedents. There are consequences, the Spirit of promise answers to faith, faith is both anointed and sealed in the believer, faith works by love, love labours by faith, faith looks out with hope, and hope maketh not ashamed, because the love of God is shed abroad in our hearts by the Holy Ghost given unto us. The just lives by faith, he takes up the daily cross by faith, he takes up arms in the perpetual war against fallen nature by faith, he lays hold on the shield of faith in the fight of faith continually against the flesh, faith is the victory that overcomes the world, the flesh, and the devil, all worldliness, and the whole of worldly religion. Oh, yes, faith has consequences.

Faith is the fruit of the work of the Spirit, and whilst a singular, distinct fruit, it is not the only fruit. All the work of the Spirit accompanies, as it precedes, and as it follows, saving faith. Moreover the Spirit *himself* is known to faith: that is not saving faith, but damnable presumption, that knows no indwelling of the Holy Spirit of promise; he, himself, indwells the believer. That divine Person is known, and made known, and known inwardly, wherever true faith subsists: it must be so, for that same Person of the Spirit is he through whom the poor soul was brought to believe, and, without that same Spirit continually indwelling, continually inbreathing, continually quickening faith, it would be found to be false faith, it would be choked, it would wither and die. He is called *the Spirit of faith*, and if the just shall live by faith, it is only because faith lives and is kept alive by the Spirit of life from God perpetually indwelling all who are really brought to saving faith. Faith can *never* be separated from the Person of the Spirit: he begets, feeds, sustains, and ensures the continuance of faith, and, without him and his work, all is spurious and empty.

Faith is not apart from the gospel. That is, the *doctrine* of the gospel. Those who have no doctrine, who despise doctrine, actually trumpet their false faith, their carnal presumption. Faith, however, comes by hearing, and hearing by the word of God. Not the dead letter: the living ministry. 'How shall they believe in him of whom they have not heard? And how

shall they hear without a *preacher*? And how shall they
preach, *except they be sent*? As it is written, How beautiful are
the feet of them'—the sent feet, the spiritual feet—'that preach
the gospel of peace, and bring glad tidings of good things!'
Rom. 10:14,15. These things are in the doctrine of the gospel
of Christ, and these preachers are the ministers of Christ,
and by these in their sent preaching, and by these alone, *the
Spirit of Christ inworks faith in the hearers through the evangel.*

Faith is not, and cannot be, isolated from Christ, in his own
Person. That is, *in the gospel*. It is the gospel that enshrines
and makes Christ known, in the doctrine of it. 'I am not
ashamed of the gospel of Christ, for IT is the power of God
unto salvation to every one that believeth.' Many, if not
most, whilst professing faith in Christ, *have no knowledge of
him, and consequently no belief in him, as he is revealed in the
pure doctrine of the gospel.* 'But of him are ye in Christ Jesus,
who of God is made unto us wisdom, both righteousness,
sanctification, and redemption', I Cor. 1:30. There is in the
gospel a full and complete doctrine of Christ, his Person and
his work: what he has done, what he is doing, and what he
will do. This is called the apostles' doctrine, and the early
saints continued steadfastly in it. This is nothing to do with
human tradition, clerical theology, so-called 'bible training'
or religious education. It is the doctrine of Christ, and except
faith be in Christ as revealed, preached, and taught by this
original apostolic truth, in the sum of it, it is all empty claims,
all vain presumption, all sand. Faith cannot be disassociated
from Christ in his doctrine, in the gospel, whatever claims
there may be made as to knowing him, or whoever makes
them: I say, faith cannot be disassociated from the doctrine,
without which everything disintegrates into vain boasting,
light as air.

Neither can faith be disassociated from the Father. It is the
Father who reveals the Son, and without this revelation, he
cannot be seen spiritually nor believed upon. 'Blessed art
thou, Simon Bar-jona: for flesh and blood hath not revealed

it unto thee, but my Father which is in heaven.' 'No man can come to me, except the Father, which hath sent me, draw him.' And, if they are not drawn—which drawing Jesus says comes from the Father alone—how can they believe in him? It is 'Of *God*' that 'ye are in Christ Jesus.' Faith itself is the gift of God, not of works, lest any man should boast. It is the work of God that ye believe, who by him do believe.

This is the faith of God's elect, for 'It is God that justifieth', God that hath dealt to every man the measure of faith, and God who reveals his Son, draws to him, and commands and quickens faith in every one that believeth. As to all other spurious claims, false faith, and empty presumption, void of this work of God, he saith, 'Ye therefore believe not, because ye are not of my sheep.' His sheep, given to him by the Father before the world was, are brought to him in time, to whom he is revealed and by whom they believe. Immediately, seeing the Son and believing upon him, they are united in one Spirit to worship the Father: 'For the Father seeketh such to worship him', and this follows from faith in the Son. Hence, faith cannot be disassociated from God, nor from the worship of the Father. There is an essential, indissoluble connection.

Faith therefore can never be isolated from God, from the work of God, from God in three Persons, from the work of divine Persons, from Father, Son, and Holy Ghost. It cannot be isolated from the Person of the Holy Spirit, nor from the work of the Spirit as a whole. It is never isolated from all that grace works in the soul. Nor is it to be isolated from the doctrine of Christ as that by which the Spirit reveals the Son so as to quicken faith in Christ.

Faith is not a thing that can be isolated from the word of truth, the gospel of our salvation, it is brought in by these very things, because it comes through hearing and hearing by the word of God. An invented Christ of sentiment without this solid and sound foundation is nothing but a dream, just as imagined 'faith' in such a dream is nothing but presumption. All such dreaming is a substitute for the faith, a substitute for the Christian religion, and a substitute for the reality of Christ. Real faith, saving faith, however, can *never be isolated from the divine Persons, the divine work, and the divine word that initiate, accompany, and fulfil it*, and which give true, saving faith its nature, character, and validity.

(iii) It is not of man

Observe, Heb. 12:2, 'Christ is the *author*' as well as the 'finisher of our faith.' Furthermore Peter informs us, II Pet. 1:1, that the saints had '*obtained* like precious faith' with the apostles, and if they 'obtained' it, then it was not through themselves, or their own persuasions, but from God. As Paul says in another place, Rom. 12:3, 'God hath *dealt* to every man the measure of faith.' Hence, Jn. 6:29, it cannot be the work of the soul, or the work of man, or of the dead letter, or the work of mere preachers; no, '*This is the work of God*, that ye believe.' And if not, Jn. 10:26, 'Ye believe not, because ye are not of my sheep.' For, Acts 13:48, 'As many as were ordained to eternal life believed', and none other. Hence, speaking of the saints, the apostle says, Acts 18:27, These are they 'which have believed *through grace*.' So Peter explains, 'The faith *which is by him* hath given this man wholeness', Acts 3:16. 'For by grace are ye saved through faith; and that'—namely, faith—'not of yourselves: *it* is the gift of God: not of works, lest any man should boast', Eph. 2:8,9. This is called, Titus 1:1, 'The faith of God's elect', that is, of those poor creatures whom 'God *hath chosen* to be rich in faith', Jas. 2:5.

Now, if of God, then not of man; and if of God in man, then of the power of God within. This is called, II Thess. 1:11, 'The work of faith with power', and hence, he that hath it is 'full of the Holy Ghost and of faith', the two being inseparable, and the latter springing from the former, Acts 11:24. For our faith 'should not stand in the wisdom of men, but in the power of God', if it is to stand at all, I Cor. 2:5. Hence it is said, faith being wrought of the Spirit within, 'Having the same *Spirit* of faith', II Cor. 4:13. Those who are void of this power, and empty of that Spirit, make a vain profession, but the truth is 'Therefore they could not believe, because he hath blinded their eyes, and hardened their hearts.' It is true, 'The election hath obtained it.' But it is equally true 'the rest were blinded.' How? 'God hath'—mark that, *God* hath—'given them'—*given* them, observe—'a spirit of slumber, eyes that they should not see, and ears that they should not hear; unto this day', Rom. 11:7,8.

And will any contend that faith is a mere human exercise, latent in the will of man? Faith is *of God, and not of man,* and whoso denies it, hath denied the faith, and is worse than an infidel, defying the most high God, and rebelling against the Almighty, doing despite to the Spirit of grace. As to us, we own in the fear of God that we are of those, I Pet. 1:21, 'Who *by him* do believe in God', and hence fall on our faces and confess, I Tim. 3:9, that such divine inworking is nothing other than 'the mystery of the faith'.

(iv) It is not one act

Indeed, it is not an act at all, it is a *quality.* It is the issue of life, quickening, converting, divine life, which is continuous in its springing forth, and increasing in its flow. How can something that springs from life, one with it, be a single act? 'The just shall *live* by faith.' The truth is, that in the new testament there was an anxious, earnest, serious, heartfelt and wholehearted concern, even unto tears, for the continuance of *living faith* because time had revealed *how many who had begun, and begun with far more than one act, had afterwards fallen away.* I Tim. 4:1, 'Some shall *depart* from the faith.' Lk. 8:13, 'These *for a while* believe'; after which, I Tim. 5:12, they 'cast off their *first* faith'. They had it at first, the same, it appeared, as that of others. But they cast it off afterwards. What anxious apostolic labours, therefore, followed the beginning of the work of faith, manifesting itself in prayers, vigils, fastings, labours of a quality at which modern evangelicalism is utterly astonished, and which it dismissively scorns and disdains as quite unnecessary. Yet the apostle cried, wept, groaned, sighed and interceded with anxiety, 'Lest ye have believed in vain', being satisfied with nothing short of a living, growing, quickened faith constantly in evidence in all the saints and in the whole assembly.

This concern in the apostolic labourers did not, and could not, bring into question the election of God, or the perfection of Christ's redemption: *but it did not presume upon it.* The apostolic ministry looked for the vital marks of God's elect, and laboured for them, knowing that it was these issues of life that showed those for whom Christ had died: that this quickened, vital spring was the mark of the faith of God's elect. Moreover the earnest early ministers knew that *first faith*, the beginning of faith, could not be counted a mark *unless it continued in life and increase.* And in many cases, *it did not.* Many became, II Tim. 3:8, 'Reprobate concerning the faith', though not concerning dead presumption. Certain, I Tim. 1:19, 'had made shipwreck of their faith.' Indeed, 'Though one had all faith', I Cor. 13:2, it was nothing worth, without the issues of that life from which true, saving faith sprang. Thus the apostles travailed, warning every man, presuming upon nothing, lest, I Cor. 15:14, 'Our preaching be vain, and your faith also vain.' The rather they laboured that those that had begun should be of 'those that believe *to the saving of the soul*', Heb. 10:39, rather than such as 'draw back unto perdition', knowing that they, and they alone, would inherit, who 'continued in the faith grounded and settled', Col. 1:23.

So the ministers of Jesus Christ pray for us, Lk. 22:32, in the spirit of Christ, 'that our faith fail not', and send to us in their absence, I Thess. 3:5, 'To know your faith, lest by some means the tempter have tempted you, and our labour be in vain.' Let us therefore labour to enter into that rest of faith, lest any man fall after the same example of unbelief as those whose carcases, littering the wilderness, remained a memorial for evermore, a dreadful testimony of their departure from the living God.

God forbid that his servants must needs be sent to us saying, 'Ye did run well, who hath hindered you?' Or should have to lament, 'Have I bestowed so much labour in vain?' Know, therefore, that faith is no mere profession of the dead letter, nor a single act, neither an incident, *but a vital spring*, so that faith without the issue of living works is dead: faith springs up, bears fruit, and he that hath it, grows in it, for, now, together with hope and love, faith *abideth*.

(v) Faith is not a condition

That is, it is not a condition of salvation. Salvation was fully effected before new testament faith was called for. Faith therefore believes in an effected salvation. A salvation that had already been accomplished. It must be so: it is an eternal salvation, and Christ is the author of it, Heb. 5:9. Redemption is complete without faith: faith comes in to believe in a completed redemption previously outwrought: 'For thou wast slain, and hast redeemed us to God by thy blood.' This was what redeemed all who were to be redeemed: *his* being slain, and the efficacy before God of *his* blood. That secured redemption. We believe that. But our believing neither adds to it, nor subtracts from it. True faith, divinely wrought, simply brings to light those whom Christ had *already* redeemed by his blood.

The same with righteousness: righteousness, by which the faithful are justified, had already been wrought. 'He brought in everlasting righteousness.' That is, when he died. How can you add to that, or put a condition to it? If that were necessary it could not have been termed 'everlasting', for in such a case it would have depended on the fulfilment of conditions yet to come. But it did not. It was unconditional. All that remained was for that divine righteousness to be imputed. Not *completed!* It was completed. Then, it is imputed. Hence, faith is not a condition of salvation, redemption, justification, or of any such thing, because everything already, unconditionally, had been completed for the salvation of all the elect *before* they were brought to faith. Thereafter, *when* they were brought to faith, that completed work was what they believed. This is called 'The faith of God's elect', and it is the evidence of those whom Christ redeemed, God justified, and for whom the work of salvation was divinely concluded. All who believe *anything else* have not the faith of God's elect, but a presumption of their own devising, an invention of false shepherds.

It is not that God had wrought a general salvation, and, seeing this, we add to it our faith to make it applicable. It is not that we believe, and then God confers his favours upon us. That would be a salvation conditional upon faith, and, if so, faith would become that without which salvation, however wrought, would be otherwise ineffectual. But the truth is, God favoured Abraham and his seed, and did so from eternity, having predestinated the heirs of promise to sonship, *even before he wrought their complete salvation.* After he *had* wrought it, then faith followed, believing that he had already accomplished all that he had said. God said to Abraham, 'Surely blessing I will bless thee, and multiplying I will multiply thee', and confirmed it with an oath. He swore by himself to save every chosen vessel of mercy, and to do so by himself, his own arm bringing near his righteousness, salvation being of the LORD, owing nothing to man. Hence he saith in Moses, 'I will have mercy on whom I will have mercy.' So God, purposing mercy to helpless wretches, afterwards effected their eternal redemption by Jesus Christ. Only then does he quicken them by the Holy Ghost, converting them, thus bringing them to faith in Jesus Christ.

A conditional salvation is of man's initiative, but saving faith is of God's gift. Everything, in truth, is God's initiative. From eternity. In time. And to everlasting. From eternity God chose his people in Christ, naming the election, predestinating the elect to the place of sonship before the foundation of the world. In time, God sent forth his Son, made of a woman, made under the law, that he might redeem those that were under the law. And he did redeem them, by the blood of his cross, which redemption was completed by his death. The crucifixion brought in everlasting righteousness. His blood wrought eternal salvation. To everlasting this is so: otherwise the words 'eternal redemption', and, 'everlasting righteousness', have no meaning. Hence it is said, 'Whom he justified, them he also glorified.' *Then*. He secured them for glory *then*, he established them to everlasting *then*; that is, he did it when Christ died.

There is no question of a general work for all mankind, available to all—and hence effectual to none!—yet conditional upon so-called 'faith'. But such is the Arminian scheme. After thus destroying the foundations of the righteous, the Arminians have the impudence to talk of 'the eternal security of the believer'! What security? The security of the strength of the withered arm of free will, of the condescension of man's heart to believe? 'No, no', they say, 'the security of salvation.' Then if it is only salvation that gives them security, and not their so-called 'faith', why does not that same salvation— which they say was wrought for all—save all? If it is only salvation that secures, not faith, all mankind should be as secure as they are! With their scheme of general redemption and universal salvation it follows that they should be saved who never believed in their whole lives, and who died in impenitence! That is, if general salvation is their eternal security, which, they say, was wrought for everybody.

The fact is, these Arminians trust in a lie, and really confide in themselves that they are righteous. They make and believe a lie by their erroneous system of heresy in which they trust, prating about a salvation, a justification, a redemption, a 'finished work' done for all mankind, offered to all, but made good only when men believe it. But how can it be a 'finished work', as they say it is, if believing *be a condition of it*? Then it is not finished, or effectual, to anyone, without their contribution. If so, IT IS NO FINISHED WORK. They say it is, but in reality, they do not believe in a finished work, they believe in *completing* a 'finished' work! Then, 'faith' as they call it, is their whole security.

If it is finished for all mankind, and if what is finished is the work of salvation, then, by definition, all mankind must and shall be saved by it, and so universalism is found to be true after all. 'No', they say, 'unbelievers did not accept it, they did not believe.' Oh? Then, since you say the finished work was done for them as well as for you, it was not finished enough to save them. And if not, why should it be finished enough to save you? The finished work *we* believe is that Christ effectually redeemed, actually purchased, finally justified, unconditionally saved, at the cross, so that he *completed*, finished saving, all his own, and none other, when he died. If he did the same work for others as that which they say saves them, *then that work must save those others, if, as they themselves say, it in itself alone is what saves them.* Then it will, and must, save all for whom it was wrought, and, if others are not brought to faith before they die, they will have to be brought to faith after they are dead! WHAT A SYSTEM!

Because they say that they believe Christ died equally for all, yet they are forced to admit that all—if not most—do not believe, then they are driven to the position that either downright infidels and impenitents will be saved after death, or, alternatively, *nothing is effectual to any*, in Christ's work of so-called 'finished' salvation, unless their 'faith' is made an essential condition of that salvation being applied. In which case, their believing makes it effectual, just as the disbelieving of others makes it ineffectual. *If so, it does not save in and of itself.* Not unless they are wrong, and it were for his elect alone. That is what we believe, because it is the gospel, and it is the truth: Christ died for all whom the Father gave to him, so as actually to effect their unconditional salvation at the cross.

Thereafter the Spirit is sent to alarm, awaken, convict, quicken, convert, bring to repentance, and call to faith *all those for whom Christ died, and none other.* Hence it is said of all other, 'Ye therefore believe not, because ye are not of my sheep.' The Holy Ghost comes to each one for whom Christ died, in due time, so as to bring to faith those already purchased, that they might believe exactly this doctrine, called 'the doctrine of Christ', the truth of the gospel, just as their faith, like precious faith with the apostles, is called 'the faith of God's elect'.

The finished work was therefore wrought for all *the elect.* All *the sheep.* If in this sense it were for all *the world,* all *the goats,* then all would believe, for all certainly *shall* believe for whom Christ died. That the world does not believe, that the goats are not brought to faith, is proof positive against this vile error. There never was, and there never could be, a 'finished work', in terms of a 'general redemption' for all mankind, conditional upon belief, because the one is utterly contradicted by the other. Hence, they are found out to be liars, and worse, who propagate and hold such vile heresy in the name of the Lord.

It follows that just as important as 'belief', indeed, even more important, is WHAT is believed! As vital as is the *subject of faith,* even more vital, is THE OBJECT OF FAITH. What is faith's object? A general redemption for all mankind? If it is really *redemption* that these Arminians mean, and their calling it a '*finished work*' implies so, then all the world, the whole of mankind, must be saved by it. However, because all who ever shall be saved, were saved at the cross, and are in consequence

brought to faith, THE VERY FACT THAT ALL MEN HAVE NOT FAITH
SHOWS THAT CHRIST DID NOT DIE TO REDEEM THE WORLD, OR TO
JUSTIFY THE WHOLE OF MANKIND, BUT ONLY THOSE GIVEN TO HIM
OF HIS FATHER.

Hence to admit that both believers and unbelievers are in
the world—and who can deny it?—is in itself to deny general
redemption, given that the word 'redemption' is made to mean
what it says. If these Arminians will assert general redemption,
let them tell us, since they say redemption is a finished work,
Why then do not all believe? Or is God incapable of bringing all to
faith? If he is incapable, who is supposed to be Almighty, then
such supposed impotence must also bring into question the
matter of whether Christ's finished work for them will also fall
to the ground! Or perhaps God will yet save them, after death,
without their having professed faith during their lifetime?

That is, according to these Arminians, universalism may
yet prove to be true, namely, that God will save all mankind
by Christ's death, irrespective of faith, or of belief in the
gospel, or of how men lived, or died, raising all to bliss, and
denying every word ever uttered in the bible about faith, or
about the last judgment, or about heaven and hell.

See where their blind folly, or, rather, rebellious perversity,
brings these 'evangelicals', as such Arminians like to style
themselves. It brings them to universalism. At this they cry
out, however, from the thick depths of the dense fog of that
ignorance under which they are obscured: 'We deny universalism.' But if they deny universalism—the dream that all
mankind will be saved universally after death, despite everything—I say, if they deny universalism, yet obstinately hold
to a general redemption for all mankind, which they assert is
a 'finished work', then *either all men must be brought to faith*—
which, manifestly, *they are not—or else their denial is rubbish.*
Hence they deceive themselves, and all their hearers, as-
serting that which, when they hear it themselves, they are
FORCED TO DENY!

At this they gnash their teeth. For they know that, being driven, they have been pressed back upon their old false refuge, namely, that Christ wrought a general redemption for all, effectual only to those that believe. *Then that general work was not, and is not, finished. That is, redemption is not finished.* It requires 'faith' as they call it, to make it effectual, namely , to finish it. If so, Christ alone does not redeem, no, they must add their essential endorsement to his work, which they style 'faith', in order to make that redemption effectual. Some finished work! Hence, *their working* makes redemption effectual *for some*, and the *lack of working*, makes the very same redemption ineffectual *for others*. Then, IT IS INEFFECTUAL IN ITSELF, and they are found out at last holding a tissue of lies in place of the everlasting gospel.

Therefore it is not the gospel that these 'evangelical' deceivers are preaching. It is not God's gospel, neither is it God's salvation, and he who has sworn to save HIS PEOPLE by HIS OWN GOSPEL, IN THE TRUTH OF IT, and none other, and nothing else, will discover the lie in the right hand of these at the day of judgment. For, since darkness is what they prefer, it ought not to surprise them that it will be to darkness, everlasting darkness, outer darkness, that they will be consigned. The more so, since it shall appear so brightly in that day that what they had wilfully, deliberately, scornfully and rebelliously obscured and hated all their lifetime, for themselves and others, WAS THE GOSPEL OF GOD, WITHOUT BELIEF IN WHICH ONE CANNOT BE SAVED IN THE DAY OF JUDGMENT.

Then why do they go on as they do? Because these self-righteous, self-justifying creatures love the applause of men, just as they cherish the flattery of the world. But what men will never applaud, and what the world will never flatter, is the election of God, and Christ's choosing a people out of the world, effectually to redeem them by his own blood in consequence: 'Therefore doth the world hate you, because I have chosen you out of the world.' This, the 'evangelical', the

Arminian, shuns like the plague, the rather perverting the gospel of God than incurring the wrath of man.

But those whom God has chosen in Christ, to whom Christ has confirmed their election of God—'Knowing, brethren beloved, your election of God'—such as those, I say, are not afraid of the world's hatred of election. Not in the least. They aver that faith is ALL OF GOD, and nothing of man, that the object of faith is wholly of God and not at all of man, and that the subject of faith is all of God and none of man. Hence they assert that faith is God's work in them, of God's initiative, on the basis of his own election, and upon the ground of the especial, particular, and precise work of Christ on the cross in actually securing their eternal redemption. In a word, they echo the words of the apostle, 'By grace are ye saved through faith; and *that* not of yourselves: it is the gift of God: not of works, lest any man should boast.'

II. WHAT PRECEDES FAITH

(i) Much precedes generally

Quite apart from that work of the Spirit of God previously opened in the inworking of salvation, namely, the alarm, awakening, and conviction, wrought by the Holy Ghost *sounding and shining* the word of God within the sinner; followed thereafter by quickening, conversion, and repentance towards God, all of which are wrought by the regenerating divine *life* of the Holy Ghost in the inner man, much precedes faith in the salvation of the sinner.

That is, much precedes generally in the work of God in saving sinners. Yes, but nothing at all precedes easy-believing or anything else in the text-persuading, man-inducing, pride-exalting system of erroneous modern evangelicalism.

112

Now therefore we are not to be fobbed off with the dead letter, the outward form of intellectual assent, or of emotional persuasion, *for none of these things bears any relation to God's salvation, or to God's outworking of salvation.* It is a needs must that we receive GOD'S OWN WORK within our own interior souls, an imperative that we experience THE POWER OF GOD upon our hearts, for this is that which leads to faith, without which any profession is of necessity spurious. Here is no change wrought by us; here is a new creation wrought by God: Father, Son, and Holy Ghost, and nothing less is to be accounted salvation: 'That your faith should not stand in the wisdom of men, but in the power of God', I Cor. 2:5.

We do not imperceptibly or gently drift into faith; we are not and cannot be pressurised into it in big meetings, under soft lights, with sweet music, and tender appeals: that can *never* precede, and it will never result in, saving faith: only deluded presumption. Nor are we brought to faith, though we may be to a carnal 'decision' under anxious old men—or women—buttonholing us with their favourite salvation texts in the corner of a gospel hall after what they fondly think of as 'the preaching'. There can be no presumptuous assuming, no pressurising the young, no putting of salvation into the mouths of the unchanged blind, deaf, dumb, palsied and dead, as it is this day. The rustle of India paper, the incanting of texts, the clutching at the dead letter: this is not salvation; and that is not faith.

There must be a preparatory work, a ploughing up of the fallow ground, a refusing to sow among thorns, a breaking of the rock in pieces. There must be an inward, spiritual, felt witness to flee from the wrath to come, to hate the flesh and the world; a rending of the veil from off the heart, leading one to groan for deliverance, to cry out for God, the living God, to appear in salvation. There must be a loathing of one's own person, a lamentation over the hardness of the heart, a being broken under the law, a coming of the commandment within the soul, a coming to the end of the law, a being slain by Moses: OH, MUCH PRECEDES, far, far, more than modern deceivers ever knew, much less wilfully forgot.

Much precedes. Just as John the baptist preceded the coming of Christ in the history of the gospel, so his ministry must precede that of Christ in the experience of the soul. The word of the Lord must come as fire and a hammer, to break the rock in pieces, before the balm of Gilead can be applied as a salve to the wounded soul. If not, what is there to heal? 'Hath not', says James 2:5, 'God chosen the poor of this world rich in faith?' Then, *their previous experience was one of penury*. For he brought them to faith, who were first reduced to poverty. And since it is a question of 'faith', it follows, this being wrought of God within those whom *he had chosen to it*, being inward, the poverty must likewise be inward, as it is written, 'Blessed are the poor in *spirit*, for theirs is the kingdom of heaven.' It is these poor that show by their condition that God has chosen them to be rich in faith, without which choice and prior work, none would ever come to believe savingly.

There must first be a removal of the rocks, a digging up of the stones, a cutting of hardened surfaces with the mattock, a furrowing by the ploughshare, a raking with the harrow, so that the gospel sowing, when it comes, be not on the wayside, nor on shallow ground, nor yet among thorns, but on good ground. That *must* precede, which prepares for the sowing. If ever men are rightly from the heart to cry unto the LORD, it must be in their trouble, and if they are to be delivered, it must be out of their distresses. But if they have no trouble, if they know no distresses, how shall they cry? Whence the trouble and distress? Such trouble and distress comes only from the preparation of the heart by the Lord. He makes his elect, whom he chooses to save, to wander in the wilderness in a solitary way; to find no city to dwell in; to be hungry and thirsty; to know soul fainting: *then*, Psalm 107:6, 'They cried unto the LORD in their trouble, and he delivered them out of their distresses.'

This first work of God, the preparation of the heart, lies in his leading of his poor people to know their condition experimentally, their trouble, their distress of soul. Only after that, when they know the plague of their heart, do they call upon the name of the LORD. Without that, they do not. And it is *his* work to bring the soul to know that it sits in darkness and the shadow of death, being bound in affliction and iron, to bring down their heart with labour, to make them fall down, and to find out that all the vain schemes of men in religion cannot deliver in practice. Then, *then*, Psalm 107:13, 'They cried unto the LORD in their trouble, and he saved them out of their distresses.'

It is not the uncircumcised ears that hear; it is not the uncircumcised heart that believes: the hard carnal heart only assures itself, flattered by deceivers in religion, falsely comforting itself in presumption by what it hears in the dead letter. 'Wherefore hear the word of the LORD, ye scornful men, that rule this people which is in Jerusalem. Because ye have said, We have made a covenant with death'—by your Arminian general redemption—'and with hell are we at agreement'—with your lightly healing the wound, cleansing the outside of the cup and platter, and whitewashing the grave with the coating of easy-believism—therefore ye say, 'When the overflowing scourge shall pass through, it shall not come unto us'—Oh, no, once saved, always saved—'for we have made lies our refuge, and under falsehood have we hid ourselves.'

'Therefore thus saith the Lord GOD: Judgment also will I lay to the line, and righteousness to the plummet: and the hail shall sweep away the refuge of lies, and the waters shall overflow the hiding place. And your covenant with death shall be disannulled, and your agreement with hell shall not stand; when the overflowing scourge shall pass through, then ye shall be trodden down by it. From the time that it goeth forth it shall take you: for morning by morning it shall pass over, by day and by night: and it shall be a vexation only to understand the report.'

This word is to the scornful men that rule this people which is in Jerusalem: that is, the leaders, ministers, clergy, pastors, elders, deacons, of the sects, divisions, denominations of Christendom, especially evangelicalism. It is to the dead fundamentalists, the carnal reformers, the self-deceived legalists, the false assurers, the deceitful evangelists, the artful charismatics, the easy-believing brethren, that scorn the word of the Lord, that despise the truth that God has wrought redemption for his people. For it is his prerogative and his alone, not only to outwork, but also to apply salvation by his own mighty power, in an inward and spiritual way, sending from on high those preachers whom he himself endues with the power of the Holy Ghost. This is that salvation which alone shall stand in the day of judgment.

For, behold, all these blind guides, and their blind followers, blundering out of the ditch, go to meet God in judgment with a lie in their right hand, and vanity in their mouths, and with a profession as light as air. These, these are the scornful men that rule this people that is in Jerusalem, that have made a covenant with death, who are in agreement with hell; who have made lies their refuge, and who have hid themselves under falsehood. But none of them shall stand. These are they who thought that God was altogether such an one as themselves, but they shall find that he is not.

For these believe with the carnal heart, they hear with the fleshly ear, they are uncircumcised in heart and ears, they lightly heal the wound, they daub the wall with untempered mortar, they garnish the sepulchres of the prophets, but they themselves are like graves, full of dead men's bones and all uncleanness. They make clean by an evangelical profession the outside of the cup and platter but within they are full of extortion and filth. These are an abomination to the Lord, and their counsel shall not stand, nor the wicked in the congregation of the righteous.

God will have no hearing but through circumcised ears; no believing but from a circumcised heart. This spiritual circumcision must take place in the heart and ears, prior to believing, that his people might be brought to true and saving faith. 'For he is not a Jew'—nor a believer—'which is one outwardly', as they are, whose uncircumcised hearts profess to believe, and whose mouths assent to texts, supposing this will pass for faith. Faith? Not so. 'Neither is that circumcision which is outward in the flesh.' Oh, no. The heart must be changed, before it can believe, 'For with the *heart* man believeth unto righteousness.' 'But he is a Jew'— and a heart believer—'which is one inwardly; and circumcision is that of the heart'—that must take place, *that* circumcision, before man can believe with the heart, acceptably unto God—'of the heart, in the spirit, and not in the letter: whose praise is not of men, but of God.' Then how can these believe, which love the praise of man, and live for it, and receive honour one of another?

'Circumcise therefore the foreskin of your heart, and be no more stiffnecked', Deut. 10:16. 'Ye stiffnecked, and uncircumcised in heart and ears, ye do always resist the Holy Ghost: as your fathers did, so do ye', Acts 7:51. And the prophet Jeremiah saith to the unbelieving Jews, 'Circumcise yourselves to the LORD, and take away the foreskins of your heart, ye men of Judah and inhabitants of Jerusalem: lest my fury come forth like fire, and burn that none can quench it', Jer. 4:4.

For none can believe—only sound out a hollow pretence, a false faith, an empty presumption, intellectual assent, easy-believism, a complacent compliance—*but none of these is faith* —none, none can believe from an uncircumcised heart. One can believe the letter; but the apostle says, circumcision is of the *heart*, in the *Spirit*, and *not* in the *letter*. The mind, the intellect, the affections, the emotions, the will, the volition, the conscience, the convictions, can get at the LETTER, from a HARD UNCIRCUMCISED HEART. The conscience can stoutly

117

protest 'I verily thought that I OUGHT to do many things contrary to the name of Jesus', whilst still outwardly professing Christ in a carnal religion which is utterly void of the Spirit, and of his inward working.

But the SPIRIT does a preceding work in faith, to bring to faith, and, without it, all is vain presumption. There *must* be a preparatory work of God, or ever GOD gives saving faith. Oh, MUCH PRECEDES GENERALLY, such as *taking away the hard, unspiritual, carnal, unexperimental, leathery foreskin of the heart.* Then, when the SPIRIT does this preceding work, that shall come to pass which is written, Deut. 30:6, 'THE LORD THY GOD will circumcise thine heart, that thou mayest live.' And live by BELIEVING, for, 'The just shall LIVE BY FAITH'. Therefore, circumcision of heart, *wrought of the* LORD THY GOD, must and shall precede in the heart of every true believer.

Many will storm and rage against this sound doctrine; as it was in the beginning, is now, and ever shall be. For this, they slew the prophets, stoned the apostles, burnt the martyrs. Why? *Because it showed up their false, shallow, and worldly religion.* These many—always a majority—killed the seers, crucified the Lord, stoned Stephen, and hounded Paul. They will be ready to this day to praise the stopping short on the far side Jordan, admiring all false faith, and each light healing of the wound of the daughter of Jerusalem. They will flatter, smarm, and applaud a letter-learned profession as much as a honeyed, cloying committal, to make both twofold more the children of hell than themselves.

But these many, this majority, hold no sound divinity, no right doctrine; they compass heaven and earth to make their proselytes, false disciples, easy-believers; they call them forward, give them an assurance of salvation for the muttering and peeping of a text, sign up their name on a card, and at once acquit the unbelief of the worldly; the apostasy of popery; the falling away of Protestantism; the froth of the Charismatic delusion; and the vile stink of putrid Arminianism. They sound their praise at the make-believe patterns of Brethrenism; just as they clap their hands for the shallow charade of so-called reformed fundamentalism. They assure those whom they persuade, that if they say, 'Jesus, Jesus' and 'Lord, Lord', all will be safe, all is well, all will be opened unto you: BUT IT IS ALL LIES.

It is the solemn and awful truth that the vast majority of evangelicals, falsely so-called, have fallen away from the doctrine of that gospel, the belief in which brings salvation; instead, carried away with Arminianism, they have a Jesus without a gospel, a Spirit without the truth, and a God without a will of his own. In consequence, they prophesy lies in the name of the Lord. They have wilfully departed from the old paths, and have removed the ancient landmarks, forsaking sound divinity, being removed from that which marks out, and looks for, all the work of faith with power, all the power which works faith, and all the preceding stages and signs leading to saving faith, together with the doctrine thereof. I say, because modern evangelicalism—whether loose, liberal charismatics, or dry letter-learned 'bible believers'—*alike forsake the inward work of the Spirit in salvation*, ESPECIALLY AS IT PERTAINS TO THE PREPARATORY WORK PRECEDING FAITH, AND SAVING FAITH ITSELF, therefore they show themselves to be the children of those that despised the prophets, and persecuted Christ and his apostles, even such as spare not now to revile us who show them the right way of the Lord.

For these are the heirs of those who cried 'Peace, peace', when, saith God, There is no peace. Oh, yes, they will confirm multitudes in a false faith; they will assure the uncircumcised in heart that the words of the dead letter are wholly acceptable for salvation with God; they will flatter with their lips and subscribe with their hand to every fleshly 'committal', as they call it. But Paul testifies against them to their teeth, declaring that the faith of God's elect is the opposite of the false faith of these, because the elect are those 'Whose praise is not of men, but of God', and Jesus saith 'How can ye believe, which receive honour one of another?' Indeed the Saviour testifies of their false hope, saying, 'That which is highly esteemed among men is abomination in the sight of God.'

For the praise which is not of men, but of God, esteems nothing short of the interior work of the Holy Ghost in salvation, commencing with, and looking for, that alarm, that awakening, that conviction, that quickening, that conversion, and that repentance towards God which leads to and brings in SAVING FAITH. These blind guides do not: you know they do not: to a man, modern evangelicals neither look for, nor require, nor preach up such divine necessities: *they do the very opposite.* Why? Because their praise is not of God, but of men. But God looks from heaven for the heart that is circumcised by the Spirit; for that inward religion; that interior spirituality; *in a word, for all that brings in true, saving faith, with all the sound, preceding marks thereof.*

Oh, yes, much precedes faith generally. And here we have shown, as in the fear of God, with great plainness of speech, as declaring, and not shunning to declare, the whole counsel of God, here, I say, we have shown that work, that preceding work, that work that is not of man, but of God: Father, Son, and Holy Ghost. And this is the work that shall stand. Nothing else stands. But this shall stand for ever. This is built upon rock. But all refuges of lies shall be swept away. Because they are built upon sand.

(ii) Much precedes particularly

A deep, other-worldly seriousness, a shunning the company of man, an earnest, single-minded zeal that resolutely refuses the word of man in religion, and cries, cries, Oh, cries out for every word from God! There is an abhorrence, a detestation, of the attempts of those who lightly heal the wound, a cry from the heart not only for God himself to heal, but to open the wound still further, to pierce to the bottom, to cut to the root of the matter, not to spare, but to perform all the work of God with power, no matter the groaning, the pain, the distress and the terrible soul-trouble and affliction this brings on.

There is, immediately preceding faith, an utter, helpless, meek, wholehearted justification of God in all his judgments, a soul-melting, heart-breaking, agreement with every stroke of the rod, every arrow stuck in the conscience, every condemnation of the law, every reproach of the gospel, every wound from the blow of God's hand: how grateful the soul is, even in the midst of all this chastisement: melted.

There is an utter rejection, a hearty abomination, of all the modern, chaffy, light, and airy trifling with scripture, whilst there appears a solemn, God-fearing, earnest crying after the Saviour, a heart-broken crying after God, a groaning, a weeping, and a sighing after the work of the Spirit. This is accompanied by an intent searching after the sense of eternity, after real spiritual experience, after deep divine impressions upon the soul. Now, these things, these frames, immediately precede faith. Whoso hath these, 'Thou art not far from the kingdom of God.'

There is a yearning for the company of those who really have had an experimental dealing directly with God, a craving for their prayers, a searching out of their experiences. Withal, there is an abominating of false religion, an abhorrence of the world and its things, a withering scorn against those who accuse the soul of morbid introspection, of being influenced by dreadful preachers, whose wicked lives they say they can easily demonstrate with letters, and Gashmu saith it. All these the soul at the gates of Zion soon detects, and utterly abominates, seeing they are the children of those who spoke evil of the prophets, and slandered the Lord Jesus, scandalizing the apostles with their lying fables.

All these are dismissed with horror, for the soul near to faith recognises the workers of iniquity who would warn of subjective disorder, of unhealthy feelings: those who tell the soul to shake it all off, that it is not a matter of feelings: just take God at his word, that this is all the influence of that dreadful man and his awful doctrine, turning the world upside down, and Tobias and Sanballat and the Babylonian Free Press have reported it. No, no, do not listen to the terrible man, he will bewitch you with oratory: listen to *us*, trust the dead letter, whatever your heart and conscience may say to you, and no matter the plain truth of the doctrine of the gospel. By this the soul about to be delivered by the power of God knows that they plead for self-persuasion the far side Jordan. He knows instinctively that these have not entered into rest. They have persuaded themselves, and in their false zeal would persuade others of the bare letter, without the Spirit; they would cry, Stand on the bible. But stand is what the poor soul cannot do for his very life: he is the slain of the Lord, a thing about which these liars know nothing, and is fallen on his face before the altar of God, groaning, If I perish, I perish.

By 'Stand on the bible', they mean, Convince themselves of texts chosen by them, and applied to themselves in free will, 'claiming' this promise and that without a single inward witness of the Spirit, or the least vestige of a title to any one promise or text in the whole scripture. 'Oh', says the labouring soul, 'Depart from me, all ye workers of iniquity: God brought on this state, that I know, and *neither you, nor anyone else, can deliver me from it!*' 'What you ask', says the soul, 'is that I quench my convictions, grieve the Spirit, ignore the language of my heart, and refuse the urgings of my conscience; and all this *by denying his alarms; going back to the sleep of death; despising his convictions; spurning every quickening motion; turning myself backward; and putting on again the old carnal mind, which is enmity against God: this you do,* BY URGING ME TO SHRUG OFF EVERY INTERIOR SENSATION, ALL THE LEADING WITHIN

OF THE SPIRIT, DEMANDING THAT I RUSH TO THE LETTER AND
PROFESS IT IN THE FLESH, ALTOGETHER LIKE YOURSELVES!'

'God forbid!' says the soul, 'God convicted me, and led me
into the POWER of convicting texts, and GOD SHALL JUSTIFY
ME, THE SAME SPIRIT LEADING ME INTO THE POWER OF JUSTI-
FYING TEXTS. He himself shall guide my heart into the savour
of salvation, witnessing to the truth *within my own soul.* Not
you false prophets, but the *interior motions of the Holy Ghost,
these have smitten me, and slain me by the sword of the Lord,* AND
ONLY THAT SAME SPIRIT SHALL LEAD ME INTO ALL THE TRUTH
THAT REMAINS TO BE EXPERIMENTALLY BROUGHT HOME TO MY
HEART. He shall justify me, he shall heal me, *not with descriptions
of salvation* BUT WITH THE SALVATION WHICH THE DESCRIPTIONS
FIT: And what do you hypocrites know of that?'

From all of which it is evident that he in whom faith comes
to a true birth has many bitter and sore soul-travails, even
from the conception, the growth, and the delivery of it into a
full grown heart-belief and open confession. These labours of
the soul are utterly detested by those presumptuous and
arrogant hypocrites who steal the promises, comforts, and
scriptures belonging to the experimental, so as to apply what
they have stolen in self-will to their own hard and unchanged
hearts. *Because such persons never had this soul travail, this
anguish of heart, this profound inworking of conviction. And
because in their consciences they know that such a work of God in
others has eluded them, they are bitter with envy, and would, if
they could, kill and destroy this true faith wrought of God in the
poor and needy, whilst it is yet in the womb, before ever it comes to
the birth.*

These persecutors, so specious, mild, and loving to all the
world, and all the worldly religious, show the same malice to
the children of faith, as Herod showed to the Child of promise.
This false-faith fraternity seeks to obliterate the coming seed
of Christ. Like Cain, it slays its brother: 'And wherefore slew

he him? Because his own works were evil, and his brother's righteous.' The works of the one were wrought by the arm of the flesh, and the faith of the other was wrought by the power of God. So, slaying his brother, false faith would then steal from God that word which is in the Spirit's prerogative to apply to all the heirs of faith so as to bring them to true belief. So we see that 'he that was born after the flesh persecuted him that was born after the Spirit.'

And, since they cannot quench the Spirit's mighty influences in those whom God has determined to bring to the birth, and to saving faith, at any one stage, they therefore heap the work with ridicule, deriding it as being not only unnecessary, but downright unhealthy, the meanwhile stealing both the words and promises of God in the letter of them, when God intended them for none but those of that circumcised heart upon which alone he writes and inscribes this divine work. But on these bondchildren will go, persecuting the freeborn sons, even in the birth-days, seeking to confound the poor soul whilst yet he remains under darkness, much as did Job's comforters of old time.

They shoot out the lip, they puff at the child of promise, they say, 'Aha, Aha', and at the slightest slip or even appearance of a fall, rejoice and dance, crying, 'So would we have it!' But all springs from bitter envy, *because God never did the work to or for them*, that he does in his elect. For they know in their hearts that all their profession is outward in the flesh, all their rejoicing is of that brittle short-lived kind which 'Anon with joy receiveth it', and all their faith is of the sort of which Jesus testified 'which for a while believe'. Because their hearts were never prepared by God, as good ground, from the beginning. They are shallow. All their deeds are done for to be seen of men. The root of the matter is not in them.

Of closet, inward, religion these know nothing. To the work of faith with power upon a heart divinely circumcised, they are strangers. They never travailed, hence, they bring forth nothing but wind. They know nothing of the long distresses, the sore afflictions, the birth-pangs of the true children, they are ignorant of the breath of God that bloweth where it listeth, hardly even hearing the sound thereof, and if they do hear it, gnashing their teeth with fury that it has passed them by, inventing another wind and breath after the flesh to make up for the deficiency. All this while they jealously persecute and maliciously slander those poor in spirit, the true children of God, who return not railing for railing; who, when they are reviled, revile not again; who keep still, carrying their case in secret before their Father, who shall reward them openly.

Thus it is that the children of the Father, who open not their mouths before their persecutors, who are dumb as a sheep before her shearers is dumb, cry out to God in the secret place:

> 'Our soul with scorn of those at ease
>   is filled exceedingly,
> and with the sore contempt of those
>   that proud and lofty be.'

PSALM 123:4

To faith, standing as it does, not in the lightness of the natural mind, nor in the chaffy, airy vanity of nature, nor in the flippant, casual assumption of texts on salvation, nor yet in the lip-service of a fleshly profession, standing not in these things, I say, *faith eschews all of them, saying, Get thee hence!* The soul that is true feels it so: SALVATION IS OF THE LORD, it cries!

God must give relief, it sobs; Save, Lord, or I perish, it weeps; it STRIVES to enter in at the strait gate, knowing that many shall *seek* to enter in—yes, and claim to have entered in without strife—and shall not be able. The easy-believers, these majority

125

false professors, those of carnal presumption, laugh to scorn the anguish and tribulation of striving souls. They are those who make clean the outside of the cup and platter, but whose inward part is full of ravening and wickedness. These are they who, further to their claims upon certain saving texts, know that they are rich; hence they laugh now. All men speak well of them; But, says Jesus, Woe unto them. But, says the Saviour, Blessed are ye that hunger now; blessed are ye that weep now; blessed are ye when all men shall hate you, and when they shall separate you from their company, and shall reproach you, and cast out your name as evil, for the Son of man's sake: REJOICE! LEAP FOR JOY! Your reward is great in heaven: for in like manner did their fathers to the prophets.

Why did they do that to the prophets? Because they hated the power of God that rested on them whom God had chosen, but which did not rest on those—such as themselves—whom God had not chosen. They envied the Spirit-wrought poverty, weeping, sorrow of the godly, which they could never imitate, and which was a harbinger of the doom that awaited hypocrites, testifying to the emptiness of their vain profession. But the godly rejoiced! And the godly still rejoice. For it is in answer to the Spirit-wrought conditions of poverty, weeping, mourning, meekness, hunger and thirst, seen in the Beatitudes, observed in Psalms 38; 51; 143, and many others, in answer to the pricked hearts of Acts 2, to the piercing sorrow and blindness of Saul in Acts 9, in answer to the jailor at the point of suicide in Acts 16, in answer to Peter's 'Depart from me, O Lord, for I am a sinful man' in Lk. 5, *I say, in answer to these Spirit-wrought conditions that there is bestowed the free gift of sweet relief in the Saviour's life and death, body and blood, resurrection and glory, bringing to saving faith, and giving that wonderful, felt alleviation, assuaging the terrible conditions of trouble and distress by the mercy of our Lord Jesus Christ.*

This brings justification: it brings the righteousness of faith. And this faith, justifying faith, is saving faith indeed. This sets the soul to singing; the saints shout loud for joyfulness; they are clothed with righteousness, for now the time of the jubilee has come, release is proclaimed, and God says to the soul after the long night of travail, 'MY SALVATION SHALL BE FOR EVER, AND MY RIGHTEOUSNESS SHALL NOT BE ABOLISHED', Isa. 51:6.

Now the waiting is over, as indescribable inward and spiritual relief floods the soul. What wonderful salvation, beyond words to utter, is now felt by the soul that endured such long, preceding travail, whose tribulation, whose anguished labour preceded—OH, MUCH PRECEDED: MUCH PRECEDED GENERALLY; AND MUCH MORE PRECEDED IMMEDIATELY—I say, much preceded the coming of the gift of faith by which grace reigns through righteousness unto eternal life by Jesus Christ our Lord. Amen and Amen.

III. SAVING FAITH

Saving faith is that work of God in man by which one is brought to believe the gospel of God concerning his Son for salvation, through the righteousness of God and our Saviour Jesus Christ. Anything short of this is not saving faith. Saving faith is a necessary consequence of regeneration. Regeneration creates in man that kind of life which cannot help believing: for the life of one, one cannot help but look believingly through the gospel to the Lord Jesus Christ for salvation and righteousness. The quickening of regeneration, which precedes saving faith, is that by which a man is set free from the carnal bondage and deadness of unbelief, through the spiritual issue of new and everlasting life, to be brought into the liberty of saving faith. Faith is therefore not the cause but the effect, and the necessary effect, of regeneration. The quickening of regeneration in and of itself creates life that believes. Hence, regeneration precedes belief. Given regeneration, the soul lives, and lives by faith.

Saving faith is therefore not only an effect of quickening, it is an inevitable effect: belief is the very reflex of the life that quickens; the quickened soul cannot but believe. The regenerate *have* faith, because it follows from the life: they cannot *help* believing. Faith follows of necessity, and the reason is, Christ has been revealed in the regeneration. This causes the blessed soul to embrace him, and him alone, for time and eternity, for remission and redemption, for salvation and reconciliation, for justification and righteousness, for substitution and propitiation, for adoption and sonship, for ministry and service, and for church and worship.

Everything, but everything, appears in the Son of God, who has been revealed to the soul, who is seen within, and seen spiritually. It is the glorious light of Christ's countenance that God has commanded to shine within in the heart, whereupon one confesses him joyfully. At this, Christ says in response, 'Blessed art thou, for flesh and blood hath not revealed it, but my Father, which is in heaven.' Now to the soul Christ is all in all, bringing in that melted, meek, and childlike trust, which the soul has and must have continually, in life and in death, in time and in eternity, on earth and in heaven, for this world and the next, world without end, Amen.

Now, saving faith has three aspects, the one negative, the other positive, and the last constant.

(i) The negative aspect of faith

Faith rejects certain things. It is not just positive. What faith rejects is exemplified by the father of the faithful, Abraham. This is carefully explained by the apostle Paul in Romans 4:18-25. 'Who against hope believed in hope, that he might become the father of many nations; according to that which was spoken, So shall thy seed be. And being not weak in faith, he considered not his own body now dead, when he was about an hundred years old, neither yet the deadness of Sara's womb.' He believed in hope, but it was *against* hope! Abraham had received God's promise of life, that he should conceive seed. But this was against hope. Reason affirmed that such a promise was ridiculous; it was impossible. First, because of his own great age, for he was walking as a dead man, 'his body now dead', and second, because of his barren and ancient wife, no better than he, for her womb was quite dead. But despite this hopeless position, Abraham hoped against hope: to him these things did not come into it. Death did not come into it. And if not death, then neither sin, for it was sin that had brought about death. Hence the consideration of his own, and his wife's, sin and death, might well have been a rational consideration, but Abraham did not consider it: 'he considered not his own body now dead, nor yet the deadness of Sara's womb.'

God had promised life, and to Abraham, that ruled out death. Just as it ruled out sin. Sin and death, however universal, simply did not count to the man who had received God's promise of life: he believed God, and the negative of that was, he would not even consider the working of nature, the inevitability of sin and death. To him, God's promise of life soared over all, no matter how irrational, how impossible, it all seemed to be. God's promise was the thing that was immutable, not the obstacles to it; the promise of life transcended all, in consequence of which Abraham's faith refused to consider any possibility of the failure of that promise. He simply refused to consider it. He rejected it. That is the negative of faith, and it is true of every heir of promise, of all Abraham's seed by faith, whether Jew or Gentile.

Again, 'He staggered not at the promise of God through unbelief', verse 20. Unbelief would have viewed the impossibility of the promise ever being fulfilled unless natural law were superseded, the strongest possible realities overcome, the certain consequence of sin negated, and the universality and inevitability of death dismissed: impossible! But to faith these things were not impossible. Rationality, law, certainty, inevitability, were not things that staggered Abraham's faith. Calmly contemplating them, he staggered not. He rejected them as having any bearing in this matter. How was that? Because of the promise of God: because such a promise, from such a God, swept all aside.

Hence, 'He staggered not through unbelief.' He would not accept unbelief. He rejected it. This comes first. It is negative. Any considerations borne of natural certainty, of lawful inevitability, are not worthy of consideration, and faith does not consider them. Any logical sequences that have always occurred, and apparently always will occur, and seemingly must occur, are mere small dust in the balance. That is, *once God had made promise*. Then, such things do not stagger faith. Faith negates them. Belief rejects them. 'Abraham staggered not at the promise of God through unbelief.'

That is the *negative* of faith. Faith negates, rejects things, first. It refuses to credit certain things, it will not even consider them as relevant, even though otherwise they would be inevitable. Faith refuses all the reasons in the world, every rationale on earth, all that natural law predicates: such things do not stagger it: faith staggers not through unbelief, no, not when God has once made known, and made known by interior revelation, his own promise. Then, faith rejects *everything* that questions that promise. It negates the wrong sort of hope, earthly hope, as being against the promise of God: Abraham hoped *against* hope. He was against, he rejected, natural hope: all his hope was in God, what God would do, it was spiritual hope. No, faith does not, and it cannot, stagger at natural laws, facts, criteria, consequences, so-called balanced judgments. It negates them. It rejects them. That is the negative of faith. And it comes first.

This negative of faith in practice involves two principles:

(a) The first principle: renunciation of one's own righteousness

This was most conspicuous in Abraham, who 'believed God, and it was counted unto him for righteousness.' If so, it follows that Abraham was fully dissuaded of any idea of his own righteousness, to which he would have had to attain by his own works. He rejected his own works for righteousness, he was dissuaded of his own godliness, he knew that he was too ungodly to attain to righteousness by works. 'But to him that worketh not'—for righteousness—'but believeth on him that justifieth the ungodly'—and therefore was persuaded of his own ungodliness and absence of all righteousness—'his faith is counted for righteousness', Romans 4:5.

Now that was exactly the case with Abraham: having no righteousness, having no strength to work righteousness, being fully dissuaded of any remote idea of any righteousness of his own, he cast himself upon God to impute to him a righteousness not his own, that thereby he might be justified. 'And he believed in the LORD, and he counted it to him for righteousness', Genesis 15:6. That is, for imputed righteousness, a righteousness wrought of God and reckoned to Abraham as his own, although he had had nothing to do with it. It had been wrought outside of himself. It was *this* righteousness which should be put to believing Abraham's account before the throne of God's justice in heaven. That is what Abraham believed. He believed in *imputed* righteousness. But to believe it, first, he had to be fully dissuaded of the very idea of having any righteousness of his own. And so it was.

And so it must be with saving faith. One must heartily, inwardly, and with a divine certainty, in a spirit of humility, be dissuaded from every notion that one could ever have any righteousness of one's own. Furthermore such a man must plainly, honestly, and openly confess it to be so, in a way which hates that wherein before he trusted, that is, hates and abominates the very idea that there there could be any vestige of good in him, of which God might approve. Now, renouncing all self-righteousness, hating and abhorring it, 'counting it but dung', the man roundly condemns self-righteousness, curses it, and owns it to be both treacherous and false.

Moreover, without sanctimonious or contrived airs, without affected mysticism or fanaticism, without opinionated or sectarian notions, without religious dogma or traditional theories, but from a soul-melted, heart-broken, trembling and contrite spirit, the man owns himself to be full of iniquity, incorrigibly sinful, steeped in corruption and all unrighteousness. He knows himself to be incapable at any time of any one good work, devoid of any inward or outward virtue towards God, destitute and wanting in every good word and work, rather in a condition of bankruptcy and debt, and with a state of heart altogether alien and contrary to God.

Such a man is utterly broken down before God. He is helplessly in bondage to the interior workings of inbred sin, so that he knows with the profoundest conviction borne of inward divine teaching that it is altogether beyond his power to obtain, claim, deserve, or otherwise lay hold upon either, firstly, the remission of his sins for the whole of his past life, or, secondly, the possibility of any righteous living or future virtue in his remaining days, so as to please God. Indeed, his language, his heart language, is this: 'So then they that are in the flesh cannot please God', Rom. 8:8.

Firstly then, the man knows that he cannot obtain, claim, lay hold upon, or ever of himself hope for, the remission of sins, no, not one least sin, whether it be the sin of ommission or commission, whether the sin of heart, mind, affection, direction, intention, outward action, inward volition, interior motive, or of bodily action. No, no remission for such a wretched man: all is condemned, and condemned in his own sight, whether of religion towards God, or charity before men, whether of holiness or righteousness, whether legal or evangelical, the mouth is stopped, and the man brought to a halt.

The mountain of guilt has accrued, the debt has accumulated, the sins are undischarged, and the self-condemned sinner has nothing to pay, nowhere to hide, and not a single mitigating plea to make for the whole of the life, in every part and at every second of that life, lived even unto this present.

Secondly, such a person sees so clearly, by an inner revelation, a hidden wisdom, that there is absolutely no possibility of bettering himself, any more than there is any hope of future virtue: he perceives in the light of God that the state can only get worse in the future: that the last state will be worse than the first. It is so clear; look backward, forward, without, within: nothing bettered, but rather made worse. Age has not improved what seemed then to be a relatively childish innocence; age has simply ravished it. Maturity has not taught the soul to be straighter, but more devious. Time has not made the heart softer, but, rather, harder.

If therefore in the past the floods of worldliness gushed in, the hardness of unbelief only increased, the mountains of unatoned sin rose higher: then what hope could lie in the future? What hope of improvement, in face of such past facts, though one strove from now until the last breath in one's dying day? Nothing could atone for sin; nothing could overcome the interior condition responsible for every outward lapse; nothing could prevent the rising tide of inward pollution staining every hope, intention, or resolution blacker than that which it had hoped, intended, or resolved to improve. Of this, negatively, every soul brought to saving faith is fully persuaded. Without such a negative persuasion, that is no such thing as saving faith, but rather a damning presumption.

Thirdly, it follows that at any one time, namely, consistently at the now of the present moment, the soul utterly rejects any attempt at self-improvement, any hope of producing any penitence, much less holiness: the uttermost conviction is now settled in the inmost parts, that one can do *nothing*. The language, the constant language, of the soul is this, reiterated again and again, 'I am carnal, sold under sin'. It cries out incessantly 'The good that I would, I *cannot* do.' It cannot find it in itself to repent, better itself, reform, produce faith, no, because the soul is convinced of *inbred* sin: of innate badness in the inmost man beyond all mortal power to counter or rectify, and quite past all the help of man to remedy.

These are the deep, strong, powerful convictions that are the negatives of saving faith. These always attend, they never depart, they are the essential marks. These are the ways, paths, and landmarks by which all the heirs of promise are brought to saving faith. By these directions they learn to negate for ever and finally every vestige and concept of their own righteousness.

Neither is this muttered in some religious corner, or peeped at particular religious seasons: all these things are feelingly and openly confessed; out of the fulness of the heart the mouth speaketh; it is fearlessly made apparent, plain to all, that this is the real state, the actual condition, of the man. No one could be in any doubt about it: here is the prevailing, the ruling condition of that soul, as it pertains to the negative: there is absolute self-condemnation, and total self-condemnation, root and branch. These negative convictions, as wholehearted beliefs, feelingly, sensitively, spontaneously and unaffectedly confessed, really and truly govern the soul.

But not only does faith, in the negative, reject all notions of self-righteousness, but with this there is always allied a second negative principle, namely:

(b) The second principle: confession of God's wrath

Now, this strong principle effectually negates the lie of the serpent in the garden of Eden, that is, 'Thou shalt not surely die.' Here originated the falsehood that wrath and judgment

134

will not be executed against disobedience, because of God's love, or of special relationship, or of privilege. This lie, as a false hope, has pervaded the corrupt mind and nature of man in the Fall, just as it has been whispered continually by Satan to mankind from the beginning of the world even until this present time. But it cannot be whispered in or to the man brought to saving faith! He is thoroughly persuaded of God's judgments, of his terrible wrath, he knows the sentence of death has been passed on all mankind, he has found out the liar, who abode not in the truth, who lied from the beginning, and found him out to be false, having heard for himself the words of wrath 'Thou shalt surely die.' The man brought to saving faith has experienced in himself the truth that 'death passed upon all men, for that all have sinned'; indeed, he knows of a certainty, 'In Adam all die', and, moreover, all are under the curse. Oh, such a man is fully persuaded of God's judgments.

Faith, in the negative, owns up that the temporal judgment of God, under the law, in the ministry of condemnation and death, is not only what one deserves onself, but also what every one shall surely receive from the Judge of all the earth. Shall not the Judge of all the earth do right?

Yet for all the ingrained lie against the wrath and judgment of God in the nature of the flesh, for all the incessant whispering of Satan, the father of lies—'Thou shalt not surely die'—echoing through and from generation to generation, for all the complacent assumptions pervading multitudes of forms and channels of expression, still, superstitious fear makes unbelieving men, even in trivial events, flinch beneath expected punishments. Whereas real accident, or sudden disaster, brings the generality to cry out the very opposite to that lie which in health and prosperity sounded forth as the boast of the souls of men. But no sooner delivered from the looked-for blow, so soon does the carnal man return to his natural state.

Not so the man brought to saving faith. Here the lie has been purged out of the inmost soul, and the deceit of the tempter detected and rejected as the abominable thing which the soul hateth. At adverse providences, legal strokes, the negative of faith cries out from the heart, 'Thou art just: I have sinned.'

The carnal man is the opposite, religion or no. Disease, accident, calamity, broken health, failed business, adverse providence, old age, the curse of the law, death itself, let these approach, and at but the herald of their coming, the natural soul is filled with cringing, superstitious dread. Should these things actually strike, then the soul is filled with resentment, bitterness and enmity. Not so the man of faith; faith expects such adversity, it is just, there is no murmuring against God's providence, no fighting the Almighty: one has earned far, far more than all this, yea, infinitely more besides, and the man of faith sees it all as merciful chastisement, he justifies God. 'That thou mightest be justified when thou speakest, and clear when thou judgest.' He says, 'The LORD gave, and the LORD hath taken away.' 'In all this Job sinned not, nor charged God foolishly.'

Hence, by the man brought to saving faith, not only legal, or temporal, but evangelical, or eternal, punishment from God, is equally justified. It is fully, meekly, brokenly owned by faith—in its negative aspect—as having been fully earned, and deservedly inflicted. Not only in this life, but after death. Not only in time, but in eternity. Not only under the law, but in the gospel. Not only as come forth from the womb, but as risen from the dead. Not only under the sun, but when the sun has melted away, its elements dissolved, in the everlasting wrath and eternal fire of the world to come. All this faith owns, and shakes in anguish.

The believing soul fully acknowledges, in dust and ashes, with tears and contrition, with fear and trembling, that it deservedly stands condemned by the eternal judgment of God. Hence the soul owns that it is only right that it is under the everlasting wrath of God, and that it must and shall appear before God at the great white throne, at the great assize, in the judgment of the resurrection at the last, tremendous, day.

Faith hides not from the truth of it, it confesses, negatively, the verity that one has despised the Father, rejected the Son, resisted the Holy Ghost, refused the gospel, denied the truth, persisted in the sin of unbelief, and that therefore eternal perdition is only just and right. This the believing soul owns right well. Faith does not dismiss this: it magnifies, it enhances the truth of it. Negatively, faith not only believes it, but it does so with a soul-piercing, heart-rending intensity that feels it to the depths of one's being, trembling in every fibre at the awfulness of what one has done, and the terror of God's impending wrath that one has brought upon one's own head. The soul feels that it has committed such enormous affront, with such overwhelming impudence, that now horror and trembling take hold of one, fully warranting all the righteous judgment of God: no punishment is too great, or could ever be adequate, save it were eternal, absolute, judgment and wrath on a scale which utterly beggars the imagination.

Of course. One had sinned against *the Almighty*. Against *each divine Person*. One had sinned against *one's own mercy*. One had sinned against the one hope of salvation, *the gospel itself*. Oh, how cutting are all these negative things to the soul brought to saving faith. How just the eternal punishment appears: for sins of impudence against the incarnate Son; for sins of ignorance against the everlasting gospel; for sins of contempt against the eternal Spirit; for sins of folly against the mercy of God which endureth for ever! How one feels that one *ought* to be sunk in the lake of fire and brimstone, world without end, enduring in one's immortal soul and body those unending torments which one has justly brought down upon one's own head, and that without remission or intermission for ever and ever. Oh, whoso hath not this in the negative, whoso hath not this feelingly and heartily,

certainly hath not saving faith, but remains yet in unbelief
on the far side Jordan. The cry of the heart utterly justifies
God: the never-dying soul had through life trampled
underfoot the infinite love of the everlasting God, manifest in
the priceless blood of his beloved Son, witnessed by the
eternal Spirit: and what punishment could possibly equal
such inexpressible audacity?

What punishment? Oh, cries the soul brought to believe
the truth, Oh, unbearable punishment; endless wrath; punishment without remission, perpetually inflicted, eternal in
duration, this, this, even this is too lenient for such an one as
I am, for the heinous, the unspeakable wickedness of mine
iniquity, which has mounted up to heaven, has spilled over
into eternity, and has affronted the unbounded love of the
everlasting God.

Whosoever cannot own this negative principle, whatsoever
man hath not this as a hearty conviction, wheresoever he be
in whom this becomes not a ruling motive of his being, let
not that man think that he has come to saving faith. He has
not come so far as to the belief of devils. For, Jas. 2:19, 'The
devils also believe, and tremble.' They *know* that the wrath is
coming, and tremble. But presumptuous men do not come so
far as to the negative of faith, it does not agree with them,
they turn from it, they will have none of it, they do not
believe like that, and hence, knowing no wrath, do not
tremble. No, they have faith, as they call it, without the
negative, wrath is nothing to do with their faith, they would
rather giggle than tremble. But they will not laugh at calamity
when they fall into the lake of fire, nor will they mock at
judgment when the wrath of God comes upon them to the
uttermost. Till then, they disbelieve these negative things,
and snigger at them, for all this hoping to be saved by their
so-called 'faith'. But the devils believe also, and laugh not;
they do not snigger: they tremble. And will they be saved?
They will not. Then neither will presumptuous rebels whose
false faith comes not so far as the belief of devils.

Yet this false faith, this presumptuous easy-believism, this worse-than-devilish substitution of fleshly, worldly belief for true, saving faith, is the very inheritance of this generation from the apostate wickedness of their fathers in religion. To this dreadful delusion, the present generation of opportunist leaders, pastors, ministers, priests, besides the prolific herd of evangelists and similar blind guides, have fallen down as one man, yielding up to the carnality and worldliness of this generation, tailoring the bible—if their false and unscholarly versions can be called the bible—and cutting the cloth of the gospel to suit the fashionable dress of those congregations that provide them with a living, a platform and a certain popularity.

And why should this surprise anyone? Was it any different when God made an end of Jerusalem in the days of the prophet Jeremiah? Was it any different when God made an end of Judaism in the day of Christ? Neither shall it be any different now that God has broken off the apostate and fallen Gentile branches of Christendom, evangelical, fundamental, Brethren, reformed, and all, even as it appeared at the end of the previous dispensation, and was forewarned at the beginning of this present age, Romans 11:16-21.

Thus comes to pass in our days, the words of the prophet in their days: 'Thy prophets have seen vain and foolish things for thee: and they have not discovered thine iniquity, to turn away thy captivity; but have seen for thee false burdens and causes of banishment.' No, it was all then, and it is all now, 'Peace, peace; when there is no peace.' It is all, 'lightly healing the wound of the daughter of Jerusalem.' That is, it is all, No negative aspects of saving faith. But they have made this people to trust in a lie, supposing evangelicalism, Protestantism, fundamentalism, denominationalism, Pentecostalism, Brethrenism, the charismatic delusion, the whole system of modern religion, to be all too secure for God to judge.

But he has judged, and he does judge, and he will judge, just as to their bewildered astonishment—and the astonishment of the world—he judged an all too secure Israel. 'The kings of the earth, and all the inhabitants of the world, would not have believed that the adversary and the enemy should have entered into the gates of Jerusalem.' But they did enter, and destroyed and carried away till nothing was left, and the sole remaining prophet, Jeremiah, was carried away by the rebellious remnant, even as a captive, returning to that Egypt from which so long before their fathers had come out. Nevertheless, the prophet bore witness even to the end of his days, as you read in Jeremiah and the Lamentations.

Is it likely, then, that we shall escape, if we neglect so great salvation, which at the first began to be spoken by the Lord, and was confirmed unto the following generation of the early church by them—the apostles—that heard him? God bore those apostles witness, a witness unique to the apostolic age, both with signs and wonders, and with divers miracles, and gifts of the Holy Ghost, according to his own will. Then, seeing God bore the apostles such a witness, we ought not to neglect the great salvation spoken by them. But it has been neglected, the great mass despising and rejecting the salvation, yet pretending to be heirs to the gifts of the apostles and their ministry, blinded in their own delusions.

Therefore we ought to give the more earnest heed to the things which *we have heard*—not to the miracles and signs which accompanied those who spoke these things at the first: but to what was *preached*, to the *speech* itself, to the things *heard* —lest at any time we should let them—*them! them!*—slip. But they have been let slip, and never more so than in the case of the negative aspects of faith, without which there can be no positive saving faith at all.

Hence, if the people of our own day forsake not the sins of their fathers against the gospel, but prefer rather to continue with them to refuse the negative aspects of saving faith, let no one be deceived, as if they hold the least jot or tittle of any one positive aspect of faith. What they hold is a lie in their right hand, and with it they shall be snared, stumble, and blunder upon the dark mountains, groping for the wall like the blind, and fall in the dust, till they awake in the great resurrection to the blinding glare of that terrible judgment of which they made so light.

And, mark, to confess the negative aspects of faith is not to make some bare intellectual assent, like empty-headed parrots repeating some theological persuasion of opinion. For the whole of saving faith, negative and positive, is *inwrought*, I Cor. 12:6, 'The same God worketh all'—mark that, *all*—'in all.' In all, observe; not in *some*, in all. Then, whoso is not included amongst this 'all'—in whom 'all' is inwrought—hath less part and lot in the matter even than those devils which believe, *and tremble*.

God at the beginning, and God till the end, inworks *all* the truth, and *all* of saving faith, with *all* its preceding stages, in *all*, who are to be saved. 'All in all.' Thus the Lord adds daily to the church such as should be saved. Theories about the church, or church government, or theologies, or man's doctrines, or the assembly, or the table, or baptism, or the ground of gathering, all these things are but the exterior chaff. 'What is the chaff to the wheat, saith the Lord?' When the Holy Ghost works in the will of God to bring a sinner to saving faith, this true doctrine, of sin and judgment, is weighed right home to the heart of the inner man under the cutting operation of the sword of the Spirit, by the hammering and burning work of the word of the Lord, through the inworking power of that God who worketh all in all. 'And of the rest durst no man join himself to them.' And so it was, in the beginning.

Negatively, then, saving faith involves, firstly, the being inwardly and experimentally dissuaded, by the interior teaching of God, from all notions of one's own righteousness, or of any possibility of ever attaining to any righteousness of one's own. Secondly, the negative aspect of saving faith involves the being spiritually convinced, by the mighty inworking power of God, by the Holy Ghost powerfully operating upon the inward man, convinced, I say, of the certainty of the wrath to come, of the day of vengeance, of eternal wrath and everlasting punishment, world without end.

And this, so that the bare doctrine of scripture on these two heads is not merely read in the bible, but preached by one sent—'For how shall they believe in him of whom they have not heard? and how shall they hear without a preacher? and how shall they preach, except they be sent?' Rom. 10:14,15. Yet, though one be sent, by those sent, Christ must also speak from heaven, the Holy Ghost must inwork on earth, and the power of God must operate all in all, so that there follows in the hearers a felt, spiritual experience within of the reality of the things preached in the power of the Holy Ghost without. The truth must be so deeply inwrought that the inward man is melted, impressed, and moulded by the hearing of the word of truth from the heart.

This is to 'obey from the heart the form of doctrine delivered unto you.' This is the effect of one being sent 'for the obedience of the faith' to a place where 'the Lord hath much people in this city'. This is the bringing to light of that people, and their being brought to the light. This is the Holy Ghost bringing that people to saving faith. This is Christ building his assembly. Take these things away, or dismiss all that precedes them, or remove both negative aspects of them, then Paul will appear to have been mistaken when he reasoned of sin, righteousness, and judgment to come, and so all will enter in not by the door of the sheepfold, but climb up some other way.

But these things cannot be taken away. They are immutable truths. And those who do take them away—such as the false evangelicals and evangelists of this generation—are found out to be nothing but thieves and robbers of saving faith. But their so-called faith is unbelief. They do not believe savingly. They are the authors of their own faith. They therefore believe not, because they are not of his sheep. But all Christ's sheep, brought to saving faith, entering in through the door into the sheepfold, look unto Jesus, and own this truth: 'He is the author and the finisher of our faith', Heb. 12:2. And his authorship writes saving faith originally and by name on the heart and forehead of every one of his own sheep.

And he writes so as it is evident in all the flock, and to all the flock, that the negatives come first. Without a knowledge of the plague, there can be no experience of the cure. Without sin and judgment being inwritten, so that one believes and trembles, then all need of the cross, all necessity of Golgotha, remains but a theory in the head. But to all those brought to saving faith, to eat of the crucified flesh, and to drink of the shed blood, of the Son of man, these things become the deepest need of the soul, and the greatest necessity of the heart. Why? Because the negatives of the faith come first. 'They that be whole have no need of a physician, but they that are sick.'

And none believes he is sick—not *that* sick!—of such a dread plague, till it is made to work in him first, so as the real state of the heart is disclosed to the soul. When that happens, nothing in heaven or on earth or under the earth, nothing in this world, that world or any other world, nothing in time or eternity or in any age or any generation, nothing, no, nothing, will keep that poor, wretched, afflicted, trembling, sin-sick penitent from believing every positive truth in Christ preached by grace to the saving of his soul.

(ii) The positive aspect of faith

As in the case of the negative aspect of saving faith, so likewise with that of the positive: the apostle brings forward

Abraham, the father of the faithful, as the exemplar. Paul appeals to the inspired record—'For what saith the scripture?' Rom. 4:3—'Abraham believed God, and it was counted unto him for righteousness.'

Expounding this, showing the saving faith wrought in Abraham, the apostle Paul first of all directs the reader to this negative principle: 'To him that *worketh not*', Rom. 4:5. That is, saving faith, negatively, renounces works, it 'worketh not', it rejects any notion of righteousness by nature or by works, owning that both nature and works are thoroughly ungodly, in consequence of which the soul stands convicted under the judgment of God. In a word, saving faith is utterly dissuaded of its own righteousness, and absolutely convinced of the wrath and righteous judgment of God gone forth against it. Then, of course, of necessity, such a soul 'worketh not'. That is the negative of faith.

In parallel with this the apostle goes on to the positive principle, Rom. 4:5, 'but believeth on him that justifieth the ungodly'. Here is the ringing affirmation of saving faith; though dissuaded of one's own righteousness, though convinced of the righteous judgment of the wrath of God upon one's head, nevertheless saving faith looks up, saving faith looks up believingly, saving faith looks up despite all the negative things in which it believes, and trembles, still, saving faith looks up over all because for it all, saving faith cannot but 'believe on him that justifies *the ungodly*.'

That is what Abraham did. 'He believed God, and it was counted to him for righteousness. Now to him that worketh' —that is, that seeks, on the basis of presumed ability, assumed free will, and supposed goodness, to work out for himself a righteousness with which he hopes to approve himself before God—'to him that worketh is the reward not reckoned of grace, but of debt.' He is so good, you see, so righteous, God owes it to him: he has put God in debt to him. He thinks. 'But to him that worketh not'—how can he work? he is dissuaded of any idea of his own righteousness; and far short of seeking God's approval of his attempts to be righteous, he is persuaded that God's wrath and judgment have already gone forth against him!—'but to him that worketh not, but believeth on him that justifieth the ungodly'—here is the positive principle of faith; now follows its consequence—'his faith is counted for righteousness.'

Once more—so important is the issue of saving faith—the apostle illustrates the same thing further on in the chapter. There is a negative as well as a positive aspect. Negatively, first, Abraham's faith renounced certain considerations. 'Being not weak in faith'—he did what?—'*he considered not.*' That is the first thing about Abraham's faith, which was not weak, 'he considered not'. What did Abraham not consider? 'He considered not his own body now dead, when he was about an hundred years old, neither yet'—did he consider—'the deadness of Sarah's womb', Rom. 4:19,20.

How does this 'not considering' illustrate the negatives of faith? Because he would not consider death, or deadness, as having any bearing on what God had promised to bring to pass. Now death is the consequence of sin, 'for the wages of sin is death', Rom. 6:23, but the saving faith of Abraham considered not sin and death, that is, his own sin and death. He knew that he was sinful, namely, that he had no righteousness of his own; he knew that he was a dead man under the judgment of God: he was persuaded of that.

Saving faith does not deny these negative things for one moment. Abraham accepted that he was ungodly, he was thoroughly persuaded of it, but whilst having such negative persuasions, his saving faith soared over them all to believe that *God could, and God would, find a way to justify him despite them.* If so, he believed God would provide a righteousness, wrought out divinely outside of and apart from Abraham,

145

which, when outwrought, God would put to Abraham's account as if it were his own. Now, that is justification, that is what Abraham believed, and that is what all saving faith everywhere and in all cases whatsoever believes, wholly believes, and must believe, to warrant the name.

From which conclusions, opening up the positive aspects of saving faith—that is, what faith affirms—three principles are heartily embraced:

The first principle: Everything was laid upon Christ

Nothing is clearer to the believing soul—and by it made clear to everyone else—than the first great positive confession of saving faith. This affirmation comes from the heart, and wells up through the lips: 'For with the heart man believeth unto righteousness; and with the mouth confession is made unto salvation', Rom. 10:10. When the soul is brought to such saving belief, and when all that is within one is moved to such a confession, the heart is melted, the interior softened, and all the inward parts flow out in love at the awareness that all the righteous judgment of God so justly earned, and stored up for the day of wrath, that great day of vengeance beyond the resurrection, all, all, all has been borne by Christ at the cross!

All one's sins, the mountain of debts, all one's inbred sin, every offence is seen as having been taken away by the Saviour on the tree: everything was laid upon Christ! All that the soul had felt so deeply, so poignantly, that had pierced through the heart with such believing conviction, now with an even greater force is seen as having been the very thing which the Man of Sorrows bore on the tree, the very content of the cup which he drank to the dregs in his agony. All one's sins are now seen as having been laid upon him; he is seen to have been made sin in one's stead; upon him the curse fell, the wrath descended, and from him the righteous judgment of God was exacted, all for the very things which the soul felt so piercingly, believingly, guilty: everything was laid upon Christ.

How wonderfully the eye of faith perceives, and the hand of faith receives, this saving truth: all that negatively was felt so deeply to be such an insurmountable barrier, such an unbridgable gulf, such an impassable obstacle, such an insoluble difficulty, not only for time but also for eternity, not only within oneself but before God, all, all, all now melts away! Because all was laid to the charge of the Surety, all was put to the account of Christ. Each terrible adversity was taken up by him so as to resolve everything, but everything, that stood against the soul. Nor is this all: for it was God himself that laid everything upon Christ; God himself that charged the Surety to pay one's debts; God himself that put all to the account of Christ. And if God be for us, and for us so as not to spare his own Son, but to deliver him up for us all: then, say, who can be against us?

Henceforth therefore to the believing soul the wrath of God due to one's sins, and the vast debt owed to the law of God, is seen to have been put to the account of the Man on the felon's tree, so as actually to have been borne by the Son of man in the place of the transgressor, so as really to have become his, as if he himself were the sinner, as if he himself were the debtor, and as if he himself were the one that had transgressed. Consequently he is seen, and seen because of the operation of God upon him, as the Substitute of the believing soul in the place of accountability before the very judgment of God.

Thus was the wrath of God poured out, the fury of eternal vengeance unleashed, and the penal sentence of the law exacted: the very judgment due to the convicted sinner fell upon the spotless Substitute, now made sin, and bearing sins, just as if the Saviour were the sinner himself in the sight of

God. Eternal vengeance demanded and received the full tale from the suffering Substitute hanging upon the tree in the hours endured on the cross, in the hidden dealings of God with the Son of man, unseen by men, unrecorded at the event, invisible in the dark.

But so it was in the mysterious transaction at the cross between the Father and the Son, between Almighty God on high, and the suffering Substitute below. Jesus endured an equivalent of punishment and pain to that required from the convicted sinner by the justice of God at the bar of judgment in the endless ages of the next world: a sentence equated with the torment of the lake of fire and brimstone burning world without end, of the anguish of the undying worm in everlasting immortality, and of that bottomless pit and outer darkness of unending suffering throughout eternity to come. All, all, all was laid upon Christ, he bore it all, he waded through it all, he took it all away, he paid the price, clearing everything charged to the account of the guilty soul, and, lost in wonder, love, and praise, that is precisely what saving faith positively believes.

Faith vitally perceives, and from the very heart, that since the eternal Son of God, when he became incarnate, took human nature into union with his divine nature in the perfection and unity of his Person, it follows that at the cross, when this same Son of God was offered up, that humanity, now united and pertaining to such divinity, of necessity must have been capable of rendering so vast, so untold, so immeasurable a degree of suffering, that it could only be calculated in terms of infinity, of the eternal, and of the absolute. For that perfect humanity, now offered up, was seen as cradled in the arms of his infinite, everlasting, and absolute divinity. Before the righteous judgment at the throne of God's justice, here was suffering in behalf of all his people— yea, and suffering beyond suffering—actually commensurate with the endless torments that lay beyond death for that vast number whom he was to redeem, an endless torment which every one of them fully owns and feelingly believes to have been earned, and which all would deservedly have reaped for eternity, throughout the never-ending ages of the ages, had not the Saviour intervened, and had not God laid everything upon the one who died in their stead.

With a deeply inwrought and piercing conviction the believing soul feels to the bottom of his heart that what was laid upon Christ at the cross was what he himself would have had to have suffered after death, an endless torment stretching away beyond the judgment into everlasting infinity, to be endured in the blackness of outer darkness, world without end, without intermission, for ever and ever. How profoundly this is borne in to the consciousness of every believing soul brought of God to saving faith! The soul is cuttingly convinced, and that with a piercing awareness, of its own incalculable debt owed to the law of God, of its immeasurable accountability before the justice of God, and, above all this, of the eternal weight of wrath and judgment it has brought upon itself in its vain and light trifling with the gospel of God, even up to the very hour of being brought to saving faith.

The soul had spurned everlasting love; it had denied eternal truth; it had despised the Highest; it had defied the Almighty; it had ridiculed the prospect of infinite bliss; it had mocked the danger of unending punishment: yet the soul was immortal. Now therefore in the name of justice what else can be pronounced and brought upon its never-dying being but the inevitable consequences of its own actions? The soul must be immortal: the body may be destroyed, yes, but the soul never; withal the body shall be raised to join the never-dying soul at the resurrection. The soul *must* face immortality; the soul *perforce* shall abide continually after death, thereafter *necessarily* the soul must be possessed of a heightened consciousness beyond present calculation.

Where, how shall it then live? It had chosen in this life to live without God, and in consequence, after death, and for ever beyond it, the immortal state has been fixed by this temporal folly. What else can the end of that soul be, when once in eternity, but the opposite to that end despised in time? Not therefore, an eternity with God in glory in everlasting bliss; but inevitably an everlasting punishment with the devil in outer darkness under eternal judgment. But the believing soul, believing *this*, believes not only this, but believes and cries out also with the rapturous affirmation of saving faith: *everything was laid upon Christ!*

Now therefore behold the soul brought of God to have this witness in himself by the Holy Ghost: *everything was laid on Christ!* Here is saving faith! This weeping, this laughing, this crying, this singing, this rejoicing, this triumphant soul shouts aloud for joyfulness, falling down in worship, prostrate with joy unspeakable and full of glory, in an ecstasy beyond words at such a heart-rending, soul-melting, ravishing view of dying love at the cross: 'Even Jesus, which *delivered us from the wrath to come.*' That is, delivered all brought of God by the Holy Ghost to saving faith. Delivered them? From the wrath to come? How? Because *everything was laid upon Christ.*

Overwhelmed with everlasting love, such a soul falls into the embrace of a propitiated God; surrenders to the everlasting arms of a reconciled Father; he swoons at the feet of such a glorious Saviour; he yields up all that is within to the interior motions and inward witness of the indwelling Holy Ghost: overwhelmed! What untold easement from the burden of sins; what immeasurable relief from the law and its curse; what unspeakable deliverance from the everlasting punishment of the judgment of God! All, all has been fully honoured, and the soul justly acquitted, not only by a law magnified and made honourable, but by the very righteousness of God once so dreaded and feared, and all 'by faith in his blood'. *Everything was laid upon Christ.* He bore it all in death.

Faith

This is faith's ringing affirmation: the soul sees, and sees by faith, everything, but everything, was laid upon Christ. For oneself. That it was done for *me* is attested by such a mighty inward witness, such an immense interior surge of life, such an undeniable testimony of the Holy Ghost, such a wondrous seal to all that preceded, and much preceded, the alarm preceded, the awakening preceded, the conviction preceded, the quickening preceded, the conversion preceded, repentance preceded, the negatives of faith attended, but now all is culminated in the great, triumphant exaltation of saving faith, *Everything was laid upon Christ.*

The relief, the easement, the lifting of unbearable pressure, experienced by the believing soul under this powerful and inwrought witness of the Holy Ghost, the Spirit testifying of salvation sealed within, all, all cause the soul to 'Shout for joy', as saith the psalmist. In spirit one dances before the ark, one leaps for joyfulness, the mouth is filled with laughter, the eyes weep with gratitude; the heart swoons for meltedness; a new song fills the mouth. *Salvation*, the soul cries! *Remission*, it laughs! Oh, this is as frontlets before the eyes; as a sign upon the hand; as a fringe upon the garment; and all put there not of men, not by oneself, but of God: Oh, glory! cries the soul: *Salvation is of the LORD!*

Now the cross of Christ; now the blood of Jesus; now the triumphant resurrection and ascension; now the radiant outshining of the glory of God in the face of Jesus Christ; now the powerful doctrine of the gospel, in a word, now the truth that *all was laid upon Christ* fills the exulting soul. This truth is always before one's face; its lilting melody ever enraptures the tongue; its eyes are ever dancing for joy; its heart is ever overwhelmed with gladness, in this the day of the soul's espousals. This glorious doctrine is spoken of in one's downsitting and one's uprising; it issues forth from the mouth in one's going out and in one's coming in; it is the breathing of the lips in one's lying down and in one's rising up. It is the

151

language of the heart, and the speech of the life. It is the soul's constantly uttered testimony before man, and its continuously breathed thanksgiving before God.

The speech of such a man brought thus to saving faith stands in words which the Holy Ghost teacheth, it is expressed from the innermost depths of one's being, and the utterance thereof is clear as crystal, as gold like glass, guileless, so patently honest and sincere. At once the soul is spontaneous in its testimony, it cannot help but speak the things which it hath seen and heard, the centre, sum, and substance of which is this: *everything was laid upon Christ!* And this is no more than the lips giving vent to the fulness of the heart, for out of the fulness of the heart the mouth speaketh. In a word, with the heart man believeth unto righteousness, and with the mouth confession is made unto salvation. Now, from this follows the next great positive principle of saving faith:

The second principle: Christ took everything away

The verity that *everything was laid upon Christ* is not the end of the glorious truth that the soul brought to saving faith feels so instantly. Saving faith, perceiving by revelation all that was involved for oneself in the cross of Christ, sees in that death a full discharge and deliverance from the law. Such a soul cries 'I through the law am dead to the law!' The mouth of such an one is for ever echoing the words brought home to the heart, 'Ye are not under law, but under grace', and, 'Ye also are become dead to the law by the body of Christ.' Oh, exults the ransomed soul, then, 'We are delivered from the law, that being dead wherein we were held', Yea, saith the Spirit, 'Christ is the end of the law for righteousness to every one that believeth.' How this is written by the Holy Ghost in the heart and upon the mind of every one brought to saving faith. But it is not written in the heart, neither remotely conceived in the darkened mind, of any one single bondchild, each of whom God has given over to legal bondage and a blinding delusion.

But the truly saved soul, to the envy of every miserable legalist, the jealousy of every hypocritical Calvinist, the enmity of all who are in the flesh in religion, I say, the truly saved soul —to their bitter resentment—dances for joy at such a deliverance, such a justification from a law and commandments which neither we nor our fathers were able to keep. 'The law a rule of life?' cries the delivered soul, set free from its unbearable yoke: 'Nonsense!'

The law is a sentence of death, and nothing else, and its ministry is the ministration of death, and none other. But since *everything was laid upon Christ*, cries the delivered soul, and *Christ took everything away*, then, 'I through the law'— both magnified and made honourable through Christ's death —'am dead to the law.' Dead to the law and its curse; dead to legal bondage; dead to the old killing letter; dead to the rule of the entire legal system: 'dead to *the law!*'

The soul brought to saving faith is the soul that sees that it has not only been delivered from the curse of the law, and its condemnation, wonderful as that is; but it would all be undone, the enlightened soul sees it so clearly, all be undone, and the curse and condemnation would thunder afresh, if the law—in any form—should come in again. But it cannot come in again. It cannot get past the cross. Hence there is not merely a deliverance from the curse and condemnation of the law: one is dead to *the law itself.* Christ becomes *the end of the law* to every one taught of the Spirit and brought to the truth.

But more: faith sees that the degree of condemnation that punished and slew the crucified Saviour was not *only* measured by the law and its curse. It was that, but it was far more than that. Truly the suffering Saviour satisfied every legal demand, and met every requirement of the law, but he did much, much more than that. The law was certainly a measure, but it was very far from the only measure of what Christ should suffer to redeem the guilty sinner. God necessarily consulted that measure, judging by it what equivalent was required in the Saviour to satisfy every penal sanction against the sinner, so to transfer that sentence to the Substitute, that he might meet the law in all its rigour. But there was another, infinitely higher, price to pay, if men were to be brought to God.

This must be so. We are not brought to the law by the grace of Christ: we are brought to God. We are not brought to an earthly tabernacle, a carnal priesthood, an unrent veil, or to tables of stone concealed in the forbidden sanctuary. We are not brought to the mount Sinai, to the mediator Moses, to the Aaronic priesthood: 'For the priesthood being changed, there is made of necessity a change also of the law.' Then, what was laid upon Christ, and what he took away, must exceed the law and its rule.

Were it not so, the gospel must read 'I am not ashamed of the gospel of Christ, for therein is the righteousness of the law revealed.' Or else, 'the righteousness of Christ revealed.' But it does not so read: it reads in fact, 'I am not ashamed of the gospel of Christ, for therein is the righteousness of God revealed.' Then there is an infinitely higher rule. The puerile fiction that 'Christ kept the law for us'—instead of delivering us from it!—coupled with the inane fable that 'the law is the Christian's rule of life'*—when the law is nothing but a ministration of death—would mean that the work of Christ had brought the believer back to the law. Which law never brought, and never could bring to God. But the truth is Christ has brought the elect *from* the law that in the gospel all who believe might at last come to God himself. 'Wherefore, my brethren, ye are become dead to the law by the body of Christ; that ye should be married to another, even to him who is raised from the dead, that we should bring forth fruit

---

* Read 'Deliverance from the Law: The Westminster Confession Exploded'. See Advertising Pages.

unto God', Rom. 7:4. 'For I through the law am dead to the law, that I might live unto God', Gal. 2:19.

It follows that another, a higher, rule than that of law must be met, and was met, when everything was laid upon Christ, and when Christ took everything away. If God had limited himself to the transcript, or rule, of the law, and laid no more upon Christ than that which stood between us and the law, we would in consequence have been brought to the law. But not to God. Certainly not to God. But between the righteous rule of the law, a rule of righteousness for *man*, and the divine nature of the everlasting God—what he is in and of himself, who is, and was, and is to come, the Almighty—there is an infinite, immeasurable, inconceivable distance. And that distance is measured by another, higher, rule altogether, a rule that *only begins* when and where the rule of law ends.

Now, that divinity is the rule, quite apart from the legal rule, by which God measured what was to be laid upon Christ, and what Christ would take away at the cross, on behalf of every one brought to saving faith. Thus, saving faith brings to God: Father, Son, and Holy Ghost. Not merely to an appeased law, a silenced curse, and an unrent veil, with human priesthood ministering on earth before a distant, unknown Jehovah, whose presence remained concealed within the forbidden Holy of holies, Heb. 8:4.

In the faith, we are delivered from the law, the veil has been rent, and we have access into the holiest in the heavenly glory by the blood of Jesus, where JEHOVAH is revealed in three Persons: Father, Son, and Holy Ghost, one God, blessed for evermore; revealed, moreover, as *our* God, and *our* Father, through Jesus Christ our Lord. What rule was it that brought us so far, altogether beyond the rule of righteousness for man measured by the law given on earth, the penalty of which was borne, and deliverance from which was achieved, by Jesus Christ in the gospel? What rule? Why, the rule of the righteousness of God, a divine quality altogether apart from the rule of righteousness for man, infinitely above the law, apart from time and creation, an everlasting quality of the Godhead within himself.

It is *this* rule, the rule *of God's own nature*, that must measure the distance from an earthly law hidden in a worldly sanctuary, up to that which soars into the heavenly infinities, transcending all comprehension, penetrating the light which no man can see, or hath seen, ascending into the very heart and nature of the deity. And, such an incomprehensible distance having been divinely compassed, to take that measure down to accursed, transgressing man, so to lay all upon Christ, that he might take everything away, between the fallen creature and the most high God, *thus bringing us to God himself in his own Person.*

Here is no mere legal measure of just satisfaction to the law and its curse, rendered in suffering on the cross, to satisfy the penal rule, though this terrible price was exacted from and paid by the Saviour. Here however is *divine satisfaction* to *everlasting righteousness* that, withal, the Saviour might bring us *to God.* This is resolved by that divine attribute which measures the infinite degree in which the divine nature in itself had been offended; the degree in which divine wrath must be propitiated; the degree of distance not between man and the law, but between God and man. This is an infinite degree which defies all measure save that of *the righteousness of God,* which is precisely what is manifested in that gospel which was preached in the beginning.

Such an infinite measure as the righteousness of God, of himself, in himself, necessarily must be expressed in superlatives. It is incomprehensible, infinite, eternal, absolute. It is to the I AM that inhabiteth eternity to whom such a measure must be taken, a distance which neither Moses nor angels could remotely imagine, a distance at which they could but tremble, a distance known to God alone, a distance comprehended by none save the Almighty, the Everlasting, a distance measured by none other than the Son of God, and in no place save that of the cross at Golgotha.

Thus, because *all that* was laid upon Christ, and because he took *all that* away, the sinner is brought *to* God. Oh, what infinite measure, what an infinite measure, pressed down and running over: but this *was* the measure that was meted out to Christ. No wonder then, if this was what God spared not to inflict upon his own Son, no wonder, I say, at that punishment due for eternity from the immortal souls of those unbelievers who laughed in this life at their calamity in the next, and who despised and scorned the sufferings of that Saviour who alone could have brought them to God.

How great therefore was the price exacted from the Surety for that people for whom he put himself in bond! What infinite, incomprehensible measures of suffering were pressed upon his soul in the hours on the cross! There the Son met the righteousness of God's own nature, far and above meeting the righteousness of the law required from human nature, though both were rendered in full tale according to that divine justice which neither adds to nor subtracts from the weight and duration of the proper sentence given in the last day.

Christ not only paid the penalty of that legal rule of righteousness for man, but above all he satisfied the ever-lasting judgment of that divine rule of the righteousness of God: 'But now the righteousness of God without the law is manifested, being witnessed by the law and the prophets; even the righteousness of God which is by faith of Jesus Christ unto all and upon all them that believe.' 'That I may be found in him, not having mine own righteousness, which is of the law, but that which is through the faith of Christ, even the righteousness which is of God by faith.' 'Even as David also describeth the blessedness of the man, unto whom God imputeth righteousness without works, saying, Blessed are they whose iniquities are forgiven, and whose sins are covered. Blessed is the man to whom the Lord will not impute sin.' And this promise was not through the law—though the law was met, magnified, and made honourable by the death of Christ—but through the righteousness of faith. That is, imputed righteousness, namely, the imputed righteousness of God.

Therefore faith, saving faith, looks at the death of Christ on the cross, and sees what infinite distances were closed by that death; what immensities were resolved; what impossibilities accomplished; what mountains were removed. Faith sees what was achieved for God and man, heaven and earth: what glory was brought in; what an eternity was secured; what heights of divine righteousness kissed what depths of everlasting peace; what mercy in God enduring for ever met with what truth divine and immutable, that should know no end: what a meeting place this was! A meeting place—in the death of Christ—not only of divine justice being requited in the law of God magnified on earth, but of everlasting righteousness being satisfied before the judgment of the deity in the uttermost heights of heavenly glory.

That is what is seen by saving faith: it must be so: *it is the righteousness of faith.* Of faith. Then, it being the righteousness of God—not of the law—that is imputed to the believer, faith sees the second and infinitely greater and more profound measure that meted out the sufferings of Christ in the place of the sinner, as far, far, above the curse and punishment of the law. The righteousness of faith sees that to satisfy *that*, an infinitely greater measure taken from the very heart and nature of the deity in the heavenly glory—the innate, intrinsic, and eternal righteousness of God in himself—must have been measured down from light unapproachable, from heights immeasurable, from deity ineffable, to the bottomless depths of that sin and depravity into which, so far below the outraged righteousness of the law, sinners had sunk in their iniquity.

158

Down from eternity into time; down from the highest heavenlies into the bottomless depths; down from the everlasting divine nature of the Almighty Creator to the created human nature of the fallen and corruptible creature; down from light unapproachable to the blackness of darkness unimaginable: that was what was meted to satisfy divine righteousness, in its divinely measured exactitude, in the suffering hours of the Son of man on the cross. All was transferred to Jesus at Golgotha. He cried, 'My God, my God, why hast thou forsaken me?' And he suffered; and suffered; and suffered to death.

Now therefore faith, saving faith, sees all that distance removed. It feels by experience within itself, by the mighty witness of the Holy Ghost, the absolute victory of that atonement, and the total efficacy of that shed blood. In a word, faith sees that not only was everything laid upon Christ, but *that Christ took everything away.*

Faith feels itself sealed by that Holy Spirit of promise; secured under the imputed righteousness of God; at one with the deity in the Father and the Son; already in heavenly glory; belonging to the world to come; passed from death unto life; translated into the kingdom; even now in and of eternity! Faith, saving faith, is assured of all, and for this cause, that nothing could be more certain than that all that stood between itself in that accursed fallen state of nature, and those heavenly, divine, and eternal heights to which it has now been brought, has been taken away in Christ. Indeed, this was what was precisely measured out to the suffering Substitute upon the tree, and hence faith concludes that, seeing the total acceptance of the substitution, *all was taken away, and taken away world without end.* Amen.

This leads naturally to the third positive principle of faith, that is, saving faith, the faith of God's elect:

The third principle: Everything stands in Christ

Faith perceives the grace that God has freely given to us, not solely in laying everything to the charge of the Surety, nor yet alone in causing that Surety to achieve a full discharge from all that stood against us, and between us and God, but above all this in the abundance of love that the Father hath bestowed upon us, that we should be called the children of God. Faith grasps the wonderful truth that 'the Father himself loveth you', seeing that it is he that chose us in Christ, that it is of God that we are in Christ Jesus, that God and the Father has given us such a place of acceptance in Christ, such nearness of access to himself, that where the Son is—having borne our sins; being raised from the dead; ascended into his presence; seated in the throne of his glory—*there we are also*: 'Accepted in the beloved'.

Everything, for faith, is in Christ. Everything is taken up with where *he is*: 'that where I am, there ye may be also.' It is not a question of where we are, rationally or terrestrially. It is a question of where *he* is, actually and celestially. And however irrational and disorientated we may appear to be in the reasoning of men, it is none the less true, 'That where I am, there ye may be also.' 'Accepted in the beloved.'

Then we are not of the earth, neither of this world, nor of the present creation. Reason may say that we are, but things utterly beyond the grasp of reason have taken place in Christ, and faith has received them gladly, and believed them. Reason predicates every position upon the sight of visible and repetitive criteria, but God has wrought what is neither visible, nor repetitive, neither is it outwardly comprehensible: but *it is none the less real*. Far more real than anything in this vain world, or in transient time. God has put Christ to death for our sins; God has laid upon him the wrath to come according to the measure of his own righteousness; God has raised him —and if so us in him—from death and the grave; God has called him—and if so, us in him—to the throne of heavenly glory: faith *sees* this, and believes it, and reckons it: *everything stands in Christ.*

The believing soul receives and confesses the truth that God has made him to be sin for us, who knew no sin, that we might become the righteousness of God in him. That what Christ is in divine righteousness, before the throne of glory, in light unapproachable, becomes that place which, through the death of the cross, has been gained by him and in him for all his people. It is really believed: that we are the righteousness of God in him; that what he is in divine righteousness, as raised and glorified, we are in him.

The distance, and the full measure of that distance, both the cause of it in the sin of man, and the reason for it in the righteousness of God, was laid upon the Surety to resolve and remove at the cross: he did resolve it; he did remove it. The measure of the victory of the death of Christ for his believing people is seen in the place where Christ now sits on behalf of that people in glory. That place is the believer's place, and for this reason: *everything stands in Christ.*

This is openly confessed. Not only that Christ bore our sins in dying for us, but that Christ took away sin and we died in him. Not only that Christ was buried, but that we were buried with him. Not only that he was raised, but that we were raised as one with him. Not only that he is seated in heavenly places, but that in Christ we are ascended and seated together with him. This is not hidden, nor shut between the pages of a bible, nor stored on a mental shelf in the memory to be shuffled out at the appropriate meeting: *it is a reality, more than breath, more than life, more than necessary food, drink, or raiment,* to the soul brought to saving faith: *everything is in Christ.*

He is our life. For we are dead, and our life is hid with Christ in God. When Christ, who is our life, shall appear, then shall we also appear with him in glory. This is the life of faith, and all who are brought to saving faith live it, and live it together. For the just shall live by faith.

How openly saving faith is confessed! It is not furtively shut up and hidden in a corner, it is confessed and plainly manifested, so that it is obvious to the whole world that its very heavenliness and spirituality have become the ruling principles of the life of faith. The heart completely embraces that *everything is in Christ*, because one was *identified with him at the cross in his substitution*, and, moreover, *that identification never ceased after his death, burial, resurrection, and ascension.* Nor will it cease in the resurrection and the inheritance of the everlasting glory in the world to come. I say, the heart embraces this completely, and the *ecclesia* which Christ builds, his assembly, embraces this completely, so as to enter entirely into the rest that remains for the people of God.

It is indeed a revelation of Christ as alive, as above, yet within, as he with whom one is actually in union in light, life and love, really formed in the inner man so that his presence is consciously known. This makes the soul to cry out at the present time in the end of the world, as did they in the beginning of the gospel: 'Thou art the Christ, the Son of the living God', and moreover, to gain the wondrous response: 'Blessed art thou; for flesh and blood hath not revealed it unto thee but my Father which is in heaven'.

Here faith is seen to be the answer of the soul to God's interior work of revelation. Not to the revelation of scripture, observe, although the scriptures are revelation, written revelation, but of themselves, and by bare belief in them, none comes to saving faith. 'The letter killeth, but the Spirit giveth life.' The scribes and the Pharisees had the scriptures, and diligently searched them, believing them implicitly: 'Ye search the scriptures', said Jesus to them, testifying what was no more than the truth of their diligence, and where their 'faith' lay. It lay in the dead letter of scripture. And, saith he, 'Ye will not come to *me* that ye might have life.' Why not? Why would they not come? Because there was no work of God in them. All their religion was of their own doing.

But there is a people in whom God has wrought: he has commanded the alarm, awakened them, they have been convicted by him, he has quickened them, his power has converted them, they have been granted repentance unto life, and saving faith is not what they have wrought towards him by the letter, but what he has wrought in them by the Spirit. By the revelation of the Son from the Father in heaven, immediately and inwardly, by the Holy Ghost, the heart response of such a blessed people to such a heavenly inshining is what is called 'the faith of God's elect', or, in a word, Saving faith.

It is not without the word of truth, the gospel of our salvation. But under the sent preaching of that word—'how shall they hear without a preacher? And how shall they preach, except they be sent?'—lies an infinitely deeper, inward work of the Spirit of God. This glorious work stands in the heavenly revelation inshining from the Father of glory, in the interior vision of the Person of the Son of God, and in the union and communion that follow from the springing up of divine light, life, and love within. I say, such a work of God is wrought beneath the exterior sounding of that word, and lies at an infinitely more profound depth of revelation of the very reality and experience of the things which that preached word had described from the written revelation of the scriptures.

The things described in the gospel to those who were once without eyes in the dark, once without hearing in the silence, suddenly blaze with the light of the glory through the newly opened eyes of the hidden man of the heart, now thunder into the soul through the wondrously circumcised inward ears of the interior man, so as to raise the dead to life again out of the sepulchre of the soul. Thus the Person and work of Christ, once so remotely described in the preaching of the gospel, suddenly becomes vivid, vital, and clear, more real than the things that can be seen, and more certain than the things which are visible. Hence one can say, 'Now mine eye seeth thee', and, 'mine ear hast thou bored', as the voice of the Son of God, and the revelation of the Father, command life into the dead soul lying inert in the tomb of inbred sin, sealed under the gravestone of the law.

This powerful and interior operation of God within the heart brings the soul instantly to saving faith in the Person and work of Christ, set forth in that gospel which is the power of God unto salvation to every one that believeth: 'For our gospel came not unto you in word only, but also in power, and in the Holy Ghost, and in much assurance', I Thess. 1:5.

(iii) The constant aspect of faith

Not only are the just reckoned righteous by faith: they live by faith. This is the righteousness of faith, as it is written, and written three times over in the new testament, 'The just shall live by faith.' And if *live* by faith, by definition it is continuous over the lifetime, that is, the period of living. If live by faith, then it is commensurate with life, and superior to death, hence the victory cry: 'These all died in faith.' Not one of them out of it. How could they die out of it? They *lived* by it, the just *lived* by faith, to their last breath, as saith the apostle Paul, when he stared the king of terrors in the face, looking death eye to eye, 'I have fought a good fight, I have finished my course, *I have kept the faith.*' So it is that he adds, 'Henceforth there is laid up for me a crown of righteousness.'

Saving faith is both ratified and sealed by this sure testimony: it increases continually. It grows with life. It is not just a bare, stultified, detached belief in forgiveness of sins, nor even

—what rises higher than the mountain above the plain—
simply a trust in justifying righteousness, then no more. But
saving faith, that which *really* credits the remission of sins,
that which *truly* believes in justifying righteousness, I say,
saving faith grows and increases in such a way that the just
are said to live by it. Saving faith ranges through the whole of
spiritual experience; it searches out every truth; with holy
boldness saving faith penetrates the inmost sanctuary; saving
faith opens with rapt delight the hidden riches of the treasury
of the house of the Lord, rejoicing with joy unspeakable and
full of glory.

Saving faith quarters and traverses the entire heavenly
country that lies over the river Jordan; its staves are heavy
with rich fruits of the promised land; saving faith ascends
into the hill of the Lord; it goes up with a shout to mount
Zion, the feet of saving faith stand within the gates of Jerusalem,
and the face of saving faith beholds the King in his beauty.

Saving faith drives out and triumphs over all the enemies of
the Lord, within and without, leaving no area of the secret
life, or of public worship, that is not brought to the line of
righteousness, and the plummet of justice, according to the
words of God. Saving faith narrowly watches and brings home
to itself the strictest self-judgment with the most zealous
experimental spirituality. Saving faith tries the inner, the
outer, the public man, and the assembly, by the word, the
testimony, the judgment, the law, the commandments, the
precepts and the statutes of the Lord.

Saving faith sees how it is delivered lawfully from the old
law, set at liberty from the old yoke, and freed from the killing
letter. Notwithstanding, saving faith exemplifies the righteousness of the law by attending to the truth of the gospel in
a way fit to make every blind legalist—who understands
nothing whatsoever of what he says nor one single word of
what he affirms—blush for shame.

Saving faith rejoices in the truth of the gospel, seeing therein the righteousness of God revealed; saving faith delights herself in every revealed truth, every ordinance, every doctrine, tracing each beam of light radiating from the glory of God to its source shining in the face of Jesus Christ. Saving faith comprehends the truth as a whole, the gospel as an entity, the doctrine in its entirety, rightly dividing and giving proper proportion to each truth in relation to every other, seeing the whole to blaze with revelation from the glorified Son of God.

Saving faith separates from the world, comes out of the apostasy, denies all sectarianism, denominationalism and independency, utterly refusing the dismal reports of those false and unbelieving spies who say, 'Who can show us any good?' Saving faith hearkens to the voice of the Son of God, triumphs in the doctrine of the apostles, and rejoices in that which was from the beginning. Saving faith accepts no compromise, refuses men's traditions, owns no ministry, accepts no ordinance, denies any assembly, save that which equates with what was in the beginning, and stands in the present work of the Father, the Son, and the Holy Ghost.

Saving faith delights in love, takes pleasure in mercy, rejoices in kindness, cuts off him that privily slanders his neighbour, thinketh no evil, detests the talebearer, detects the false report, and sets her heart on the faithful in the land. Saving faith honours profoundly all the Person and all the work of the Son of God, delights to trace all the Person and all the operations of the Holy Ghost, and falls down in worship, worship that is in spirit and truth, before the Father, overcome with reverence and filial awe in an ecstasy of love for every gracious disclosure of the everlasting God, in the fear of the Almighty, and in the Spirit of sonship.

Saving faith is crucified to the world, reckons herself dead indeed unto sin, does not sin, abides in the eternal seed, looks for the resurrection from the dead, waits for the coming of the Lord, and hopes for the inheritance of the world to come with all the heirs of promise in everlasting glory. Saving faith comes in with the bleat of a lamb, sallies forth with the roar of a lion, goes up with the sound of a trumpet, and cries out with the shout of a king. The chariot wheels of saving faith carry the soul through life, its whirlwind bears up the soul in death, it laughs to see the last enemy destroyed by the cross of Christ, its cry of triumph rings and echoes round the vault of heaven, its thunderous praise sounds and resounds the victory cry 'O death, where is thy sting? O grave, where is thy victory?' And, at the last, falling on her face, all a-tremble, shaking with awe and overwhelming love all at once, saving faith lies prostrate before the throne of God and of the Lamb, I say, at the last, saving faith is swallowed up in glorious sight, to the ages of the ages of the everlasting glory, world without end. Amen.

Such saving faith utterly transcends the kind of 'once saved always saved' dead-letter assent that passes in Brethrenism, among dead Baptists, and generally in modern evangelicalism, for belief. Saving faith is not a static, past-tense, one-act, musty play mouldering on the dusty shelf of history, as if it were nothing other than a novel contrivance of man hopefully to insure his flesh against the future in case the preaching of the apostles should prove to be true after all. It is not one act at all. Salvation may have been effected, and it was effected, by one act of *Christ*; but one act of *ours* is not sufficient to obtain it, much less to retain it. It *is* one act of Christ, but it is *not* one act of faith. Faith *itself* is not an act at all.

The very idea of one single act of 'faith' procuring pardon is perhaps the most contemptible notion of justification by works that has ever been devised in order to debase the salvation of God. It is nothing but presumption begotten by ignorance out of wishful thinking. Faith is a living quality, not a past act. Faith is that living, present, growing, continuing, vital force respecting God in three Persons, each Person revealed in Christ, and Christ as made known in the gospel of God.

Saving faith embraces the whole life as such, and it is that which sees the absoluteness of God in all creation and every providence; it is that which continually presents the savour of Christ in a rejoicing belief in that more excellent sacrifice, far transcending all of those devised by the mind, will, or hand of man; it is that which has this testimony, that it pleases God, believing that he is, and that he is a rewarder of them that diligently seek him. Saving faith is that which is rapturously translated to glory at the end of a life walking with God; it is that which enters a spiritual ark built by Christ to the saving of his house, whilst the world perishes in unbelief and easy-believism.

Saving faith walks out of this world with contempt for its joys, baubles, toys, songs, honours, learning, entertainments, rewards, sports, riches and fame. Saving faith rears its head out of time, breathes the pure air of eternity, strains the eyes to perceive the distant world to come for which it lives, looks for a better resurrection, savours the scent of the lush green pastures of the heavenly Canaan across the river, beholds the mount of God, views the heavenly city, strives for the better country, and groans with groanings that cannot be uttered for the glory that is to be revealed at the manifestation of the children of God.

Saving faith sees him who is invisible, walks as a pilgrim and stranger out of this present evil and condemned world, gives its blessing in respect of things to come—not of things now present—gives commandment concerning its bones, seeks a better resurrection, and chooses rather to suffer affliction with the people of God than to enjoy the pleasures of sin—or treasures of this world's cities—for a season. Saving faith crosses the Red Sea of the judgment of God upon this present world, and crosses it dry shod; saving faith fears neither the wrath of the king nor the contempt of man; saving faith subdues kingdoms, works righteousness, stops the mouth of lions, and quenches the violence of the fire. Saving faith escapes the edge of the sword, is made strong out of weakness, is valiant in the fight, turns to flight the armies of the aliens, and receives her dead to life again.

Saving faith laughs through her tears when tortured, cries with joy in pain, would rather die than accept deliverance from man. Saving faith, in her love of Christ and following him alone in the steps of faith, hates father, mother, brother, sister, wife, children, yea, and her own life also, seeing one thing as needful. Saving faith endures sore trials of cruel mocking, she bears up meekly under scourging, she patiently suffers every chastising providence, seeing the hand of God in it all, yea, even unto bonds and imprisonments, revilings and slanders, torture and death, seeing beyond all that can happen in this world, and all that men and false brethren can do, a better resurrection through Jesus the forerunner, who went before, suffering such contradiction of sinners against himself, enduring the cross, despising the shame, for the joy that was set before him.

Saving faith has been, is, and will again be tempted under praise, wooed through esteem, flattered with honours, and urged by every promise that the world, and all the glory of it, likes to offer. But she will spurn it all, and not by one act, but throughout the whole of the life of faith lived by the just. Hence saving faith has been, is, and will again be hated, despised, falsified, stoned, sawn asunder, and slain by the sword. Saving faith was in times past, is at the present, and will be again in the future made destitute and homeless, wandering about in sheepskins and goatskins, afflicted, tormented, solitary in the deserts, alone on the mountains, dwelling in dens and caves of the earth.

Yet in it all this saving faith is bloody but unbowed; ridiculed but dignified; execrated but feared; persecuted yet envied;

slandered yet admired: for saving faith was, and is, and ever shall be, that of which the world, the whole world, the past world, the present world, and the future world, that of which the world in every generation, all nations, all classes, all creeds, all ages, all sorts and conditions, all religion, all Christendom, all dead-letter evangelicalism, all young, all old, all rich, all poor, all male, all female, I say, that of which the whole world is not worthy.

For this same living, enduring, continuing, vital saving faith is that by which the saints before us obtained a good report. It is that through which they have entered into their rest. Saving faith is the cause of their having believed and lived, suffered and died, who are now resting and waiting for a far more exceeding and eternal weight of glory, being with Christ, which is far, far better. In a word, saving faith is that by which they overcame all, entering into the everlasting rest that remaineth for the people of God.

Now, there are two vital and distinctive principles which mark the constant increase of saving faith:

(a) The first principle: faith's object becomes clearer, larger, and more absorbing

Faith perceives that the Spirit of truth, the Comforter, has come to glorify Christ. The Spirit takes of the things of Christ and reveals them more and more to the mind and heart of the spiritual man. Hence saving faith observes Christ as the object of constant attention, as he is revealed in the gospel by the illumination and power of the Holy Ghost. The Spirit does not speak of himself: he speaks of Christ. Christ is the truth, and the Spirit of truth glorifies him in the saints, so that their constant faith in Christ becomes progressively clearer, larger, and more absorbing.

(i) Clearer

It is like the blind man to whom Jesus gave sight: 'What seest thou?' 'I see men as trees walking.' *After that*, Jesus put his hands *again* upon his eyes *and* made him look up. Mark that, his sight was restored, but *after that*, there was an *again*; and still further, there was a *making him look up*. Then the heavenly light made everything perfectly clear: he saw 'every man clearly'. So it is in the constant progress of saving faith. Sight, under the operation of God in the gospel of Christ, looking up to the light that shines from heaven, becomes clearer and clearer. Christ is seen, and in that light every man is seen clearly.

Saving faith, like the restored sight of the blind man, does not remain where it was before: the hands of the Lord, the Spirit of truth, and the operation of God are continually at work to reveal and impart increasing heavenly light and interior progress in vision from the very first. Saving faith increases more and more: if at first it sees Moses and Elias with Jesus, the Father will becloud that vision, the Spirit will differentiate between Sinai and Zion to the heart, the hand of the Lord will touch the eyes of the understanding concerning both law and gospel, and, soon, no man will be seen save Jesus only, nor will any be heard but him alone. 'This is my beloved Son, hear him.'

The apostle hears of the faith of the saints at Ephesus, Eph. 1:15, but, according to the will of God, far from supposing that their present faith in the Lord Jesus should be a static thing, that it should merely be maintained, he knows that it should, it must, and it shall increase. Hence he straightway labours in prayer, and in the word of truth, that, building upon the saving faith granted to them at the first, they may go forward and abound. Hence he ceases not to give thanks and pray for them that 'the God of our Lord Jesus Christ, the Father of glory, may give' a heavenly, glorious increase to their present constant faith by granting further 'the spirit of wisdom and revelation in the knowledge of him: the eyes of your understanding being enlightened', Eph. 1:17,18. That is, the object of their vision must and shall become clearer and clearer to their true and saving faith.

Saving faith, as looking unto Jesus, its author and finisher, not only walks by faith, it increases, it breaks into a stride, it runs with patience the race set before it. Saving faith does not sit down looking back at its author, it looks up at its author, the meanwhile constantly running forward whilst beholding its finisher. How is this? Because as both author and finisher Christ is continually being revealed to the heart by the Holy Ghost which is given unto us. Christ is set down, but faith is to stand up. Christ is at rest, but faith is to walk. Christ is seated in glory, but faith is to run to meet him at his coming. 'Go ye out to meet him.' And the nearer we run in ascending the steps of faith to the light that shines from heaven above the brightness of the sun, the clearer the object becomes, and the more the words penetrate, 'I am Jesus', both Lord and Christ.

Thus the believer runs on, and so the Son of God becomes ever clearer to the heavenly vision, at last being enfolded in the arms of faith, as the mouth pours out the praises of the heart: 'Lord, now lettest thou thy servant depart in peace, according to thy word: for mine eyes have seen thy salvation.' Now, now, the race is run, the crown is in the grasp, and, if so, the distance is closed, saving faith enters into the joy of her Lord, crying, 'But now mine eye seeth thee'. And what can I more say? What, save, 'The half hath not been told me.' It must be so. Meantime, saving faith can testify of a truth, of vision that becomes clearer and clearer, all the while drawing nearer and nearer: 'And we beheld his glory.'

(ii) Larger

The object of faith, beheld by saving faith with unwavering gaze, even the Son of God, becomes increasing great—greater and greater—in the eyes of saving faith. Job, in the midst of his afflictions, had great faith in Christ, saying, 'I know that my Redeemer liveth.' But at the end of his long trials and sore afflictions he saw that same Redeemer in a way hardly dreamed of hitherto, shining in so much brighter a vision, so much larger a concept, that thus he compares his previous view, 'I have heard of thee by the hearing of the ear'—that is, the hearing of faith; yes, but the eye of faith sees the object of belief increasingly larger in his glory—'but *now* mine eye seeth thee.' And the effect of how personally, how *selfishly* one had limited the vision of the Lord to one's own needs, as opposed to his objective greatness, always affects saving faith in the same way: 'Wherefore I abhor myself, and repent in dust and ashes', Job 42:5,6.

This appears in the case of Daniel, a man greatly beloved. By faith Daniel refused the unclean food of Nebuchadnezzar, not fearing the wrath of the king. By faith he saw visions and interpreted dreams. By faith Daniel was promoted in the kingdom. By faith Daniel stopped the mouth of lions. And why? Because by faith Daniel saw in vision the King upon mount Zion, and in him he believed, opening his windows three times a day to pray towards Jerusalem. The vision of the King upon mount Zion grew larger, the King appeared ever more glorious, the vision becoming overwhelming, as with the passage of time, saving faith came nearer and nearer to that coming day upon which from the very first the heart had been fixed with such intense ardour.

Hence, even in old age, the vision of beloved Daniel's faith blazed with a light hitherto unconceived: 'Then I lifted up mine eyes, and looked, and behold a certain man clothed in linen, whose loins were girded with fine gold of Uphaz: his body also was like the beryl, and his face as the appearance of lightning, and his eyes as lamps of fire, and his arms and his feet like in colour to polished brass, and the voice of his words like the voice of a multitude.' Larger! A larger vision, a vision increased, beyond anything Daniel had seen before, or that he had dreamed, of the greatness of the One in whom he had believed from the first.

And with what effect? It is always the same, this effect upon saving faith, as the object of vision grows larger, shining not out of one's personal need of him, but out of his own glorious radiance, to a degree before unimagined. This is the effect: 'Therefore I was left alone, and saw this great vision, and there remained no strength in me: for my comeliness was turned into corruption, and I retained no strength', Dan. 10:5-9.

This is precisely reflected in the saving faith of John the apostle, whose head had leaned upon Jesus' breast, who was the beloved disciple, who—if ever any one saw Jesus—saw him most perfectly: 'Which we have heard, which we have seen with our eyes, which we have looked upon, and our hands have handled, of the Word of life', I Jn. 1:1. For who else observed so spiritually, discerned so intimately, perceived so divinely, the Person and pathway of Christ, the Son of God, as did John, in his record in the fourth gospel? And yet, for all that he saw, for all that his saving faith had embraced Christ, the Son of God, and for all that his record was to appeal to faith in setting him forth, I say, for it all, who was this that he saw in vision, incomparably larger, more immense in glory, even into his most advanced old age?

'And I turned to see the voice that spake with me. And being turned, I saw seven golden candlesticks; and in the midst of the seven candlesticks one like unto the Son of man, clothed with a garment down to the foot, and girt about the paps with a golden girdle. His head and his hairs were white like wool, as white as snow; and his eyes were as a flame of fire; and his feet like unto fine brass, as if they burned in a furnace; and his voice as the sound of many waters. And he had in his right hand seven stars: and out of his mouth went a sharp twoedged sword: and his countenance was as the sun

shineth in his strength.' Who was this? John had seen Jesus.
John had companied with Jesus. Who had been closer to him
than John? Yet when John saw the greatness, the glory, the
majesty of this tremendous vision, this glorious Person, well-
nigh defying description for his greatness, his immensity,
What? 'When I saw him, I fell at his feet as dead', Rev. 1:17.
Now, however John had seen him before, no previous vision
had caused that reaction. No: the revelation of the Son of God
became incomparably larger, in its immensity, to the increased
vision of saving faith.

The same is seen in Peter. At one time it is no more than
'Master': a mere Rabbi. But later, it is 'Depart from me, O
Lord, for I am a sinful man.' Before, it was equating Jesus with
Moses and Elias, three equals. Afterwards he confesses, 'We
were eyewitnesses of *his* Majesty.' Even when Jesus stilled the
storm, he could only say, What manner of *man* is this, that
commandeth both the winds and the waves?' Soon, however,
light breaks in from heaven, and he rises to the vision of
incomparable greatness, crying 'Thou art the Christ, the Son
of the living God.' Greater and greater he appears, as more
and more the eye of saving faith is enlightened.

So with Paul: In Acts 9:3 it is recorded 'Suddenly there
shined round about him a light from heaven.' Much later,
Acts 22:6, he says this: 'Suddenly there shone from heaven a
great light round about me'; Now, observe, it is no more 'a
light': it is 'a *great* light'. Finally, greater and greater, Paul
confesses the light that shines more and more from the
heavenly glory in the face of Jesus Christ: 'At midday, O
King, I saw in the way a light from heaven, *above the brightness of the sun*', Acts 26:13. Greater and greater. If at first the
voice from that radiant brightness testified 'I am Jesus', at the
last Paul perceived the radiance, and the glorious revelation
of the Person from whom the light shone, to be beyond all
conception: 'The blessed and only Potentate, the King of
kings, and Lord of lords; who only hath immortality, dwelling

in the light which no man can approach unto; whom no man hath seen, nor can see: to whom be honour and power everlasting. Amen.' 'Now unto the King eternal, immortal, invisible, the only wise God, be honour and glory for ever and ever. Amen.'

This same principle, that the vision of the Son of God becomes larger and larger to saving faith as it matures, appears again and again. Enoch walked with God: yes, but thereafter he was translated. Isaiah prophesied for five chapters, the word of the Lord being put in his mouth: but then he saw the Lord, high and lifted up, and his train filled the temple. Ezekiel saw the glory of the God of Israel: he prophesied for some thirty-nine chapters: then he saw that to which the glory pertained, the mystical house of God, the greatness of the dwelling place of the LORD. So with Peter: he saw Jesus: he saw the Christ the Son of the living God: but then he saw the house of God, the Stone cut without hands, and the living stones fashioned and framed by his hands, compactly built together, an holy temple unto the Lord. Paul saw the glory of Christ in a light above the brightness of the sun: decades later he saw the body of Christ, the fellowship of the mystery, and him who exceeded all that he had ever envisaged before made Head over all things to the *ecclesia*, which is *his* assembly. Greater and greater.

So with all brought to saving faith. There is not one single exception. All who are to be brought to saving faith, are brought to saving faith by that ministry sent by the commandment of the everlasting God, commanded from the glory by the mouth of the Lord Jesus Christ, to go to all nations for the obedience of faith. By such sent preachers, and such alone, the hearing of faith commences. The light of the glorious gospel shines in unto them: it is the savour of life unto life from the ministry of the gospel, in the ministers commanded of God, sent of Christ, and filled with the Holy Ghost. Thus saving faith finds its beginning in the word of the Lord.

When first the Spirit illuminates the guilty soul with the light of the Saviour, the entire vision is taken up with the view of One who freely receives and forgives sinners, who gratuitously redeems the insolvent debtor at the bar of everlasting justice, whose precious blood remits sins, covers iniquity, and blots out all unrighteousness. It is a vision of what he is for the poor sinner; what he has done, and can do, for guilty wretches; but it is not what he is *in his own Person*, it is what he is *for the lost*. Here there is a great danger of his being embraced, received, and being believed upon from nothing but selfish, and fearful causes: as nothing but an insurance against the dangers of the future. This can bring great joy, and a certain faith. 'Which for a while believe.' But afterwards these fall away.

For a while with joy they endure, rejoicing in what they have seen in the Saviour, noisily professing the same, but it never grows, the vision never becomes greater, such people always remain at the same stage. Then they have faith, but it is not *saving faith*. It is not the faith of God's elect. They are virgins, yes, they have oil in their lamps, they burble about keeping on burning. But they fall away and are lost in the end. They are fools. They have no vessel with their lamps, and hence they have not sufficient oil for the whole journey.

But saving faith loves him for what he is in himself, quite apart from what he is for oneself. Saving faith loves him for his own nature and character, quite apart from what he has done for one because of that nature and character. Saving faith gives itself to praise and worship, the word of Christ dwelling within richly in all wisdom, so that one sings to the Lord in psalms, hymns, and spiritual songs according to the word of God.* Saving faith gives itself to reading the scripture,

*Observe the unique Psalms of the Old Testament; Spiritual Songs from the Gospels; and Hymns of the New Testament. See advertising section.

to the assembly of the saints, to finding that assembly and not stopping short, to the apostolic doctrine, to being under that doctrine, and not settling for less, to the fellowship, discipline, and ordinances, under a sent ministry, in all things ordered and sure. Saving faith will not put up with less. Saving faith obeys the doctrine from the heart, hearing it expounded from the apostolic writings by living prophetic ministry, sent from Christ on high, to which it is subject with all meekness. Thus the object of faith increases, becoming more and more clear, growing larger and larger in the vision of every one that believeth.

The very words of Christ are sought out because they come from him, and likewise his deeds, works, pathway, witness and testimony. His death is pondered and searched out more and more; the sepulchre is studied; there is conformity with his death, likeness to his resurrection: the power of it is felt. The ascension is entered into inwardly, union is established, communion experienced, access obtained. His things are seen, and one's own trampled in the dust: it is *his ecclesia*, his Father's worship, God's house. *His* interests are supreme. His deity is comprehended, his humanity absorbed, the incarnation understood; his divine nature united with his human nature in one Person passes from all realms of speculation into that heavenly glory where the Holy Ghost takes of the things of Christ and reveals them within: larger and larger, greater and greater, grows the vision.

Saving faith sees Christ as the speech of God, but not as a few words out of that speech! pretentious false faith, with its noisy joy, and raucous choruses, its shallow and pathetic half-truths smarmed over with sentiment, and worked-up by artificial enthusiasm, I say, false faith grasps but a few scattered texts in its hand. But saving faith hears Christ's voice as the sound of many waters, and if so, continuously cascading, constantly thundering, ever flowing, unfailingly sounding, more and more, greater and greater. It is, 'Him that *speaketh*'—not *has spoken*—'speaketh from heaven.'

This is the Son. *He* is God's speech: appointed heir of all things; by whom he made the worlds; the brightness of his glory, the express image of his Person; he who upholds all things by the word of his power; who, having by himself purged the sins of all who are to be brought to saving faith, is set down at the right hand of the Majesty on high, the words ringing in his ears, 'Let all the angels of God worship him', and, 'Holy, holy, holy is the Lord of hosts.' There is no familiar 'you-ing' here! Here, it is Thee, and Thou, with particular distinction, according to the words and relationships of divine Persons.

Naming the deity, calling divine Persons, 'You', as opposed to 'Thee' and 'Thou'? Surely one would have thought that not even presumptuous false faith would descend to this degrading of the nature of God in three Persons, reducing what little it has apprehended of the Godhead to the familiar—and incorrect —terms of abbreviated modern human address. As opposed to *the actual translation* of the words of the Holy Ghost, of the apostles and prophets, of the church of God, and of the holy scriptures. Would even presumptuous and artificial false faith follow the madding crowd straight down this broad way of worldly craze, of blind insult, in departing from the scriptures, started by the papists, followed by the Anglicans, stampeded by the Charismatics, and drooled by the evangelicals? Would false faith? Maybe. But saving faith will not.

Saving faith will not. Of that one may be sure. For one thing the beginning of saving faith is *true*; for another, from that commencement, the vision of Christ given to saving faith becomes *greater and greater*. If so, faith becomes *more* reverent, not less. It walks in the old paths of *the* faith to glory, it does not career out of all control down the novel motorways of mass transit to hell. And the marks of saving faith are always consistent, in all ages, taking their rise from what was in the beginning, and their expression from the now despised old version of the bible that records the truth in faithful translation from the original languages. Yes, the vision of Christ becomes greater and greater.

Christ is seen by faith not only in one's need of forgiveness, but he is seen in *himself*. Now *he* fills the vision of saving faith. He fills the *ecclesia*, the body, the fulness of him that filleth all in all. That is, his fulness in the Father; the Father's fulness in him: his fulness in the Spirit; the Spirit's fulness in him: his fulness in the body; the body's fulness in him. Greater and greater. He fills heaven and earth: 'Thou compassest my path and my ways; thou hast beset me before and behind. If I ascend up into heaven, thou art there; if I make my bed in hell, behold, thou art there.' In a word, to saving faith, Christ actually, experimentally, really becomes ALL IN ALL, that in *all* things he might have the pre-eminence. To saving faith, he fills all things.

Life; death; this world; the next; time; eternity; work; rest; relations; friends; food; drink; sleep; waking; goods; money; *all is in Christ, and Christ is in all*. That is, he is all in all to growing, persevering, sanctifying, saving faith: Oh, how large, how increasingly large the vision of Christ becomes. As to what is above, 'Whom have I in heaven but thee?' As to what is below, 'There is none upon earth that I desire beside thee.' As to what is within, 'My flesh and my heart fail, but God is the strength of my heart.' As to what is ahead, 'God is my portion for ever'; so testifies the psalmist, Psalm 73.

This same saving faith brings all, all into the unity of the faith, and of the knowledge of the Son of God, from however little, however small, however simple the beginning faith; the vision of Christ increases in all whose faith is true, whose faith is saving faith. Brings all, I say, in the unity of the faith, and of the knowledge of the Son of God, unto a perfect Man, unto the measure of the stature of the fulness of Christ. That

is, unto a Christ who fills us in one body with all the fulness
of God, who fills the world to come, and the assembly, the
ecclesia, below; who fills the vision, to the very horizon, of the
saints on earth, so that their faith groweth exceedingly, even
unto the measure of the stature of the fulness of Christ, world
without end. Amen.

(iii) More absorbing

How absorbed is saving faith: as the cherubim, fixed, rapt
in gaze, all of one with the mercy seat, above and upon the
ark, so the attention of saving faith is fixed. Fixed upon the
Father; fixed upon the Son; fixed upon the Holy Ghost; fixed
upon the evangel; fixed upon the ministry; fixed upon the
saints; fixed upon the *ecclesia*, the assembly of Christ. All the
things upon which the rapturous gaze of saving faith is fixed
are but one in God. Then, saving faith despises the world,
turns from the false gospel, refuses the tampered texts and
artful devices of all erroneous versions, detests the apostasy,
abhors pseudo-evangelicalism, spurns pretend pastors, treads
down pigmy scribes, renounces the letter-learned 'reformers',
scorns the Charismatic actors. To these, who are of the world,
and whom the world hears, saving faith turns a deaf ear and
a blind eye. Of this God testifies, saying, 'Who is blind, but
my servant? or deaf as my messenger that I sent? who is blind
as he that is perfect, and blind as the LORD's servant? Seeing
many things, but thou observest not; opening the ears, but
he heareth not', Isa. 42:19,20.

The eye of saving faith is fixed upon heaven, upon the
world to come. The eye of saving faith disdains the earth, the
world that now is. The voice of joy and of salvation is in her
tabernacles, not the sound, sight, or existence of a television
set, a contemptible inconsistency of constant 'news', 'educa-
tional', and film shows not even false faith—which once
rejected the cinema!—would have tolerated so short a while
ago. Saving faith looks at Christ. Saving faith is absorbed with

Christ, saving faith is taken up with the Lord. She is ever beholding the Lord Jesus, her gaze is upon Christ Jesus, yea, saving faith views all things to Godward, all things heavenly, all things belonging to Jerusalem above, and all things pertaining to mount Zion on high.

As strengthened with might by God's Spirit in the inner man, Christ is not only believed upon, but indwelt by faith, and he in turn dwells within the believing heart. Thus the faithful, being rooted and grounded—*absorbed*—in love, comprehend with all saints what is the breadth, and length, and depth, and height of the love of Christ, which passes knowledge, being filled with all the fulness of God. The length, breadth, depth, and height of the love of God in Christ are comprehended in fulness. Here is no mere ground. Not simply a basis. Not only an area. Area is that which the multiplication of length and breadth supplies. But here is a fulness: the divine dimensions add depth and height to give volume. It is the city seen in vision by John in the revelation of Jesus Christ. Dimensions are defined, yet all pass knowledge. It is as the ark of God, in the heart of which the law is hidden in dimensions that defy analysis, covered with the cover of most fine gold, covered again with the blood of sprinkling, covered again with the perpetually absorbed gaze of the cherubim. It is as the Holy of holies, four square, in fulness of volume, bright with the glory of God.

Absorbed! This is that to which saving faith, all saving faith, and nothing but saving faith comes: absorbed in Christ; absorbed in the things of God; absorbed in the Holy Ghost and his work; absorbed in the holy city, the new Jerusalem, the heavenly country, absorbed in the worship of the Father. Absorbed in the heavenly priesthood; the glorious shewbread; the sevenfold candlestick, burning with lamps of fire; the sea of glass mingled with fire; the throne of glory; the drops of sprinkled blood following the footprints all going one way, none yet returning, disappearing through the rent veil. Absorbed!

Absorbed with the rent veil; the blood of propitiation; the clouds of incense; the ark of God, with the golden cover and the cherubim of glory; the golden pot which had manna; the tables of stone; Aaron's rod which budded; absorbed with the staves, with the shittim wood, with the shittim wood overlaid with gold, and with the gold pure all through. To saving faith, to the twenty-four elders, to all angels, to the cherubim and seraphim, to the heavenly hosts, to all eternity, to saving faith, I say, How absorbing!

The staves of the providence of God carried Christ out, up, up, up into the heavenly glory, till a cloud received him out of their sight. Mary had said, 'I saw two angels sitting, one at the head, and the other at the feet, where the body of Jesus had lain.' That was as the ark; and they were as the cherubim. Absorbed. But he is not here, absorbing as is the place where he had lain; he is risen: the staves have carried him out, out and up, up, up into the heavenly glory. The heavens have received him, as they must receive him. Oh, all heaven is absorbed. Absorbed. He takes the book, he opens the seven seals thereof. Oh, what a scene! how utterly, absolutely, totally absorbing. Eternity cannot bracket, any more than the heaven of heavens can contain, the all-absorbing glory of the Father, in the Son of his love.

There never will be time, no, nor eternity, to absorb the wonderful Person of Christ. The full greatness of the glory of the Father, seen in the Son, will ever elude the comprehension of saving faith, even to the everlasting ages. And it is right, absolutely right, that it should be so. Oh! How infinitely, infinitely absorbing. Saving faith never could, saving faith never can, and saving faith never will look at anything else, world without end. Amen.

(b) The second principle: faith itself increases, multiplies, and endures

With the edification of the body of Christ, the building up of the saints, not only faith's vision of Christ, but saving faith itself increases. There is that which 'maketh increase of the body unto the edifying of itself in love.' With nourishment supplied by the ministry, sent from above, the whole body of Christ, holding fast the Head, 'increaseth with the increase of God.' This is so of all the saints: 'having hope, when your faith is increased'; and again, 'We beseech you, brethren, that ye increase more and more.' This growth is proportionate to the edification of the saints and of the whole body of Christ. 'The word of God increased and the number of the disciples multiplied.' With divinely given ministry comes the edification of the saints, and the growth of saving faith. This growth is seen in three ways: in its increase; its multiplication; and in its perseverance.

(i) Faith increases

Though at first as a grain of mustard seed, the smallest of all the seeds, once planted in the good ground of a prepared heart, faith takes root downwards and bears fruit upwards. So, II Cor. 10, the apostle speaks without the least doubt of this divine planting, assured of the future 'When your faith is increased', for that increase must follow, in the nature of the growth and edification of the saints: 'God giveth the increase.' Not only did the saints in the apostolic times increase in faith, they lived by faith, Gal. 2:20; they hoped by faith, Gal. 5:5,6. Faith worked by love, it grew to full assurance; those that believed received the promise of the Spirit by faith; they were ever looking forward to increase of growth, called, the 'furtherance and joy of faith', Phil. 1:25.

This was to demonstrate the apostolic word, 'As ye have therefore received Christ Jesus the Lord, so walk ye in him: rooted and built up in him, and established in the faith, as ye have been taught, abounding therein with thanksgiving.' They were to 'Beware lest any man spoil them through philosophy and vain deceit, after the tradition of men, after the rudiments of the world, and not after Christ.' No, by faith they knew that they had been crucified with Christ, they had died with him, they were dead to the law by the body of Christ, they were buried with him, they had risen with him, they were seated in heavenly places in him, separated from the old man, the first man, the man of the world, delivered from this present evil age, and their life was hid with Christ in God.

Their faith abounded and increased, it grew as they were built up in the knowledge of the truth of their union with him, and in their communion with him. They came more and more experimentally into the totality of what they were in Christ, into the fulness of his work to deliver them from all below, from everything in and of this world, yea, even from time itself. Now, such edification caused their faith to grow exceedingly, as wise virgins looking and waiting for the return of the bridegroom, having their lamps burning, and oil in their vessels with their lamps.

Yet, unlike the legalists, and the prating professors of Christianity which said and did not, their transparent righteousness and holiness, endued with the Holy Ghost, infused with love, suffused with joy, brought forth from these other-worldly pilgrims of faith what empty words and pretensions about the law never brought forth from those who in mouth professed it, but in heart broke it continually. Saving faith, however, grew, and the believing saints were found to be as no others upon earth: faithful men, faithful brethren, faithful servants, faithful husbands, faithful wives, faithful children, faithful stewards, faithful ministers, and both hearers and doers of faithful words and sayings.

All this, despite those cross providences and afflictions which, whilst trying their faith, exposed the hypocrites. Despite the unfaithfulness of father, mother, brother, sister, wife, children, brethren, ministers, churches, yea, even of an apostle: they abode faithful. Abode faithful, where these very crosses tried those without the root of the matter in them, so that they fell away, but saving faith did not fall away: it had been well prepared, the ground had been prepared, it shall never fall away, it cannot fall away, no, not in the most terrible and tormenting circumstances, the most awful and dreadful afflictions. Why, when the black thunderstorms and torrential floods which obscured all have rolled over and away, and when one looks to see the crushed remnant of saving faith prostrated and bruised: it is not! Not at all. It has *grown!*

Saving faith grows in trials, it increases in the fire, it goes on, it will not decrease or dry up, it is like a tree planted by the rivers of water, that bringeth forth his fruit in his season; its leaf also shall not wither, and whatsoever it doeth shall prosper. It is ever full of sap: it shall still bring forth fruit in old age. Saving faith grows, it maintains a faithful witness, a dying witness, it cries triumphant from the flames, it shouts victory in the fire; it does not break though sawn asunder: it is a faithful martyr, it can never be crushed, and hence the apostle says in truth, II Thess. 1:3, 'Your faith groweth exceedingly.'

(ii) Faith multiplies

That faith should multiply, spreading exceedingly, was apparent from the very beginning: 'But ye shall receive power', said Jesus, 'after that the Holy Ghost is come upon you: and ye shall be witnesses unto me both in Jerusalem, and in all Judea, and in Samaria, and unto the uttermost part of the earth', Acts 1:8. And so faith multiplied, from the day in which the Holy Ghost came upon them, and the apostolic witness began its course: 'And the same day there were added unto them about three thousand souls.' 'Howbeit many of them that heard the word believed: and the number of the men was about five thousand.' 'And the word of God increased, and the number of the disciples multiplied in Jerusalem greatly; and a great company of the priests were obedient to the faith.' 'And believers were the more added to the Lord, multitudes both of men and women.' The Judeans believed. The Samaritans believed. The Ethiopian believed. Cornelius believed. The Greeks believed. The Gentiles believed. So their line went out to the world's end, their word to the ends of the earth.

The faith of the saints at Rome was spoken of throughout the whole world, Rom. 1:8. Paul *heard* of the faith of the saints at Ephesus, Eph. 1:15. The Philippians stood fast in one spirit, with one mind striving together for the faith of the gospel, Phil. 1:27. In the brethren at Colosse, the word brought forth fruit in them, *as in all the world*; the apostles prayed always for them, since they heard of their faith in Christ Jesus, and the love which they had to all the saints. The apostle henceforward would cease not to pray, preach, write, teach, labour, fast, watch, and striving according to the working which wrought in him mightily, that he might perfect that which was lacking in their faith.

The Thessalonian saints' faith grew exceedingly, and multiplied withal, spreading far and wide, and Paul thanked God for it. Their faith abounded, it added to itself, it multiplied, it increased so as to add an 'and' to itself, the apostle testifying of the faithful *and* wise; the faithful *and* beloved brethren; the faithful *and* beloved; the faithful *and* just; the faithful *and* true. No mean spread!

Thus faith was not without works, it worked by love, it was not dead, God wrought increase by it, it spread by the overreaching of its own growth: 'Joseph is a fruitful bough, even a fruitful bough by a well; whose branches run over the wall.' David said, 'I believed, therefore I spake', and Paul repeats it, with speech called the word of faith. Saving faith is like an handful of corn in the earth upon the top of the mountains—How beautiful upon the mountains are the feet of him that bringeth good tidings, that publisheth peace; that bringeth good tidings of good, that publisheth salvation; that saith unto Zion, thy God reigneth!—I say, this word of faith is like an handful of corn in the earth upon the top of the mountains; the fruit thereof shall shake like Lebanon; and they of the city shall flourish like grass of the earth.

Faith increases; faith superabounds: it adds to itself hope; it multiplies itself in love, in its very nature faith bears much fruit, hanging thick on the boughs: abundant fruit. This is to perfect that which is lacking in one's faith: there *must* be increase, there *must* be multiplication, in the very nature of saving faith. Hence faith brings forth patience; faith is ever accompanied by power: it is the work of faith with power; godly edifying, in order to edify, must be in faith. Faith removes mountains; one is shielded by faith: it is the shield of faith. The saints overcome the world by faith; they do not deny the faith; of course not: they believe it! Faith is all the work of God, it is not of ourselves, it is the gift of God, not of works, it excludes all fleshly boasting, hence it is called, Most holy faith.

We read of the communication of the saints' faith: the testimony thereof spread. We hear of the faith of the brethren being sounded abroad: there is no speech nor language where their voice is not heard. Moreover this increase multiplies itself over and over again: it abounds! it superabounds! It comes to maturity as the full assurance of faith; it enters the inheritance as the rest of faith; it finds its fulfilment in laying down its life for the brethren as the sacrifice and service of faith; and it shows its strength in its earnest contention against every error, all the enemies of Christ and of his gospel, coming to combat with untiring energy to fight the good fight of faith: Oh, there is no doubt about this: faith abounds. It superabounds. In the nature of its increase, faith multiplies.

(iii) Faith endures

The apostle Paul said as he faced death, 'I have kept the faith.' He had persevered in faith. Saving faith is certain to endure to the end. It does not, and it cannot, fall away. Saving faith, though teetering on the brink of the grave, calmly gazes down into the fresh-dug pit, it boldly stares the king of terrors in the eye, it brushes aside the rotting corruption of this mortality, it dismisses both the destroying worm and the decaying dust of death, undaunted with its last gasp, it boldly cries out, 'O death, where is thy sting? O grave, where is thy victory? Death is swallowed up in victory!'

Saving faith cannot but persevere to the end, just as it cannot but be written of all who possess it, 'These all died in faith'. Their faith was determined in divine counsels before they were born, yea, before the world was. In the eternal purpose of God they were written in the book of life of the Lamb slain from the foundation of the world, Rev. 13:8. Written, that is, whilst as yet their substance was unformed, or their members had existence, before they were fashioned in their mother's belly.

When God commanded, faith followed. That is saving faith: it cannot, cannot fail, and it shall never, never fall away. Hence, 'I have kept the faith', was spoken by Paul on behalf of every one of like precious faith. All who fail of this saying demonstrate nothing but that false faith which springs from the puny efforts of the will of the flesh, and of the will of man. These must fail, and shall fail. But saving faith cannot fail. Hence Christ testifies to the faithful by the mouth of his servant John, 'Thou hast not denied my faith'.

Saving faith is distinguished from false faith by the perseverance of the former and the withering away of the latter. Hence the admonition 'Be thou faithful *unto death* and I will give thee a crown of life.' Saving faith was one side of the line of this admonition, and was for life, and false faith was the other side of the line of this admonition, and was for death. Thus God is glorified in the vessels of mercy which he hath afore prepared unto glory; and his wrath is manifested, and his power made known, in his enduring the presumptuous boasting and vain talk of false faith in the vessels of wrath fitted to destruction. The line surely divides the twain, and each must go to his place.

There were, there are, and there shall be those who cast off their first faith, I Tim. 5:12, and the apostle assures us, their end is to be lost: 'Having damnation, because they have cast off their first faith.' Judas, once a holy apostle, full of faith, but not saving faith, becomes the father of all such in the new testament, called sons of perdition. But not at first. At first this man of the seed of Abraham, an apostle of Christ, of the chosen twelve, this man, I say, had power over all diseases, all manner of demons, power to cleanse lepers, to raise the dead, and was sent abroad to preach the gospel of the kingdom.

Judas partook of every privilege, was once enlightened, tasted of the heavenly gift, was made partaker of the Holy Ghost, tasted the good word of God, and the powers of the world to come; he was among those who handled, heard, and saw the Word of life, with them steadfastly confessing the word of faith. But, though he was numbered with the twelve holy apostles, and obtained part of this ministry, his bishoprick was for another, his money perished with him, and his faith was found to be false at the last, that had seemed so invincible at the first.

So there are those who have first faith, but not last faith. They do not persevere, theirs is not saving faith, they cannot trace in their experience the alarm, the awakening, the conviction, the quickening, the conversion, the repentance, the precedents of saving faith, nor saving faith itself. No, the short-cuts of modern evangelicalism, the pride of accursed Arminianism, the head knowledge of haughty traditionalism, the excitement of exuberant false evangelism, the snare of pseudo 'full-time service', all these their soul liketh right well; and all these will find them out and prove their destruction. 'Reprobate concerning the faith', says the apostle of all such.

190

Reprobate concerning the faith, they prove by their brittle joy, their over-excitement, their worldliness, their lack of self-control, and at last, by their deadness, the unexperimental nature of their rotten religion: in a word, they prove by their collapse that their's never was saving, persevering, but rather sham, failing faith. Saving faith always perseveres. Saving faith *holds*—and never lets go—the mystery of the faith in a good conscience. The man of saving faith is steadfast in the faith, for, 'He that endures to the end shall be saved'; and, if so, saving faith was his mercy. But those who 'anon with joy receive it', yet afterwards wither and die, 'which for a while believe', or those who believe long time, but are at last choked in old age by worldly cares and riches, these have none to blame but themselves: *They* have cast off their first faith. And since they did it, who can they blame? They have no wedding garment, and whose fault is that? Let them answer: Whose? But they are, they must be, and they shall be, speechless.

But, says the writer to the Hebrews, we are persuaded better things of you, my brethren, and things which accompany salvation, though we thus speak. Better things: better than those who entered not in because of unbelief, whose carcases fell in the wilderness. Better things: better than those who were once enlightened, who had tasted of the heavenly gift, and were made partakers of the Holy Ghost, who tasted of the good word of God, and of the powers of the world to come, who, having afterwards fallen away, were then beyond repentance.

Better things: better than the things true of those who having ardently begun in faith, afterwards drew back in coldness of unbelief: 'For it is impossible' to renew these, because, 'If any man draw back, my soul shall have no pleasure in him.' But we are not of those who draw back unto perdition. Better things: better than those who sinned wilfully after having received the knowledge of the truth, for whom remaineth no more sacrifice for sins. Better things: better things than the things pertaining to Esau, who for one morsel of meat sold his birthright; who afterwards, when he would have inherited the blessing, was rejected, finding no place for repentance, though he sought it carefully with tears.

Better things: things of the sort that pertained to the elders, who by faith obtained a good report. Things belonging to those who by faith understood that the worlds were framed by the word of God, so that things which are seen were not made of things that do appear. Better things: better than Cain. Things such as the more excellent sacrifice offered to God by Abel, offered by faith, by which he obtained witness that he was righteous, God testifying of his gifts. Things such as being translated by faith, like Enoch, that he should not see death; who was not found, for God took him. Better things: things like the opened ear of Noah, who by faith was warned of God of things not seen as yet, who was moved with fear, who prepared an ark to the saving of his house; by the which he condemned the world, and became heir of the righteousness which is by faith.

Better things: such as the things exemplified in Abraham, who by faith, when he was called to go out into a place which he should after receive for an inheritance, obeyed. And he went out, not knowing whither he went. Things pertaining to Abraham, who by faith sojourned in the land of promise, as in a strange country, dwelling in tabernacles with Isaac and Jacob, heirs with him of the same promise: for he looked for a city which hath foundations, whose builder and maker is God.

Things such as those recorded of Sara, who through faith also herself received strength to conceive seed, and was delivered of a child when she was past age, because she judged him faithful that promised. Therefore sprang there even of one, and him as good as dead, so many as the stars of the sky in multitude, and as the sand which is by the sea shore innumerable. All these died in faith, not having received the promises, but having seen them afar off, were persuaded of them, and embraced them, and confessed that they were strangers and pilgrims on the earth. For they that say such things declare plainly that they seek a country, a better country, that is, an heavenly: wherefore God is not ashamed to be called their God, for he hath prepared for them a city. Better things.

We are persuaded better things of you, my brethren, who are of the faith of God's elect, who possess like precious faith. Better things, such as those chosen by Moses, who by faith chose rather to suffer affliction with the people of God, for all the world's education, honours, and flattery, chose rather, I say, to suffer affliction with the people of God, than to enjoy the pleasures of sin for a season, esteeming the reproach of Christ greater riches than the treasures of Egypt. By faith Moses had respect unto the recompense of the reward. By faith he forsook Egypt, not fearing the wrath of the king.

Through faith Moses kept the passover, and the sprinkling of blood, lest he that destroyed the firstborn should touch them. By faith they passed through the Red Sea, as on dry land: which the Egyptians assaying to do were drowned. By faith the walls of Jericho fell down, after they were compassed about seven days. By faith the harlot Rahab perished not with them that believed not, when she had received the spies with peace. Better things. Better than anything else in the whole world, and in the whole of rotten religion, and in the entire unbelieving apostasy. Better things.

But there is a price. Yet saving faith has esteemed that price, weighing it in the balance, and has found it to be lighter than vanity, yea, altogether lighter than air. How can these things be? Because saving faith, like Moses, has 'respect unto the recompense of the reward'. And what shall I more say? for time would fail me to tell of Gideon, and of Barak, and of Samson, and of Jephthae; of David also, and of the prophets;

who through faith subdued kingdoms, wrought righteousness, obtained promises, stopped the mouth of lions, quenched the violence of fire, escaped the edge of the sword, out of weakness were made strong, waxed valiant in fight, and turned to flight the armies of the aliens.

Women received their dead raised to life again: and others were tortured, not accepting deliverance, that they might obtain a better resurrection: and others had trial of cruel mockings and scourgings, yea, moreover of bonds and imprisonment: they were stoned, they were sawn asunder, were tempted, were slain with the sword: they wandered about in sheepskins and goatskins; being destitute, afflicted, tormented; they wandered in deserts, and in mountains, and in dens and caves of the earth. For all these, every one of them, all these chose better things, for they lived by faith, and they died in faith. Of whom the world was not worthy. For the world chooses base, unbelieving things. And so does apostate, fallen, apathetic and dead Christianity.

But we are persuaded better things of you, my brethren, and things which accompany salvation, though we thus speak. And for this same cause of grace we have hope towards God that your names shall be found together with the elders who obtained a good report by faith; yea, be found, when the books are opened at the last day, in the Lamb's book of life.

From this roll shall be called the names of Abel, Enoch, Noah, Abraham, Sarah, Isaac, Jacob, Joseph, the faithful of the children of Israel, Moses, Rahab, and so great a cloud of witnesses, the seed of Abraham by faith, heirs of promise each one. Out of this book of life shall appear the record of John and of Peter, of Andrew and of Philip, of Nathanael and James, together with all the faithful disciples, of Mary and Elisabeth, of the woman of Samaria and of Mary Magdalene, of the women who by faith followed Jesus, ministering to him of their substance. The names of Paul and Barnabas, of

Silas and Titus, of Timothy and Archippus, of Stephen and Philip, of Cornelius and Philemon, together with all the elect Gentiles, once not a people, but now called the people of God, a people of faith, who walk in the faith of Abraham their father which he had yet being uncircumcised: all these. All who are of saving faith. All who are in the Lamb's book of life. 'Whose names are in the book of life', Phil. 4:3.

Here are the faithful, those brought to saving faith, called the poor in spirit, the meek, the mourners, those who weep now, those who hunger and thirst after righteousness. Here are all those hated and despised by the world, and particularly worldly religion. These are the tried, the slandered, the persecuted, the despised, the disowned, the rejected, these are the souls who sigh and cry from under the altar: these are those of saving faith.

Of them, of every single one of them, the world is not worthy. But then, they are not of the world. They love not the world, neither the things that are in the world. Christ prayed for them, and does pray for them: he prays not for the world, he has chosen them out of the world. These, for whom he prays, are of the world to come: worldly things, the carnal man, the first man, the present creation, the old law, time, the things that are visible, all have passed away for them, passed away at the cross. And they glory in the cross. It is their point of departure. The point of departure out of the world for all that be of saving faith, called pilgrims and strangers on the earth, sojourners journeying out of a condemned scene.

Now, all these died in faith. Saving faith. Saving faith with all its preparatory work, its precedents and attendants, its marks and signs following. It was not that they had received the promises, at least, not all of them, but that they saw them *afar off*. They looked not at the things which can be seen, for the things which can be seen are temporal; they looked at the things which cannot be seen, for the things which cannot be seen are eternal. They beheld him who is invisible.

They saw things *afar off*, and were persuaded of them, and confessed that they were strangers and pilgrims on the earth. That is the nature of saving faith. It is unworldly, not worldly; spiritual, not carnal; heavenly, not earthly; mysterious, not rational. In a word, it is of God, not man.

For they that say such things declare plainly that they seek a country, that is, an heavenly; and they that seek, shall find. With one voice they confess, 'I know that my Redeemer liveth, and that he shall stand at the latter day upon the earth: and though after my skin worms destroy this body, yet in my flesh shall I see God: whom I shall see for myself, and mine eyes shall behold, and not another.' They testify openly that this same Jesus, whom they at the first saw ascending up into heaven, shall so come in like manner.

'For the Lord himself shall descend from heaven with a shout, with the voice of the archangel, and with the trump of God.' He shall come in his Father's glory, and all the holy angels with him. He shall be revealed in flaming fire taking vengeance on them that know not God, and that obey not the gospel. But he shall come to be admired in all them that believe. That is, all that believe savingly. Now, that is saving faith.

At the last all these, receiving the redemption of their bodies, transformed in the glorious liberty of the children of God, with bodies like unto his glorious body, shall behold his glory. They shall, every one of them, enter into an everlasting inheritance in the holy city, the new Jerusalem, in the new heavens and the new earth, world without end, Amen.

Yet even now they behold the glorious city by faith, gleaming with gold like glass, clear as crystal, shining from just beyond the horizon, just beyond the other side of the river. Even now they see the land that is very far off. For saving faith has heavenly vision. Saving faith beholds the King in his beauty. Saving faith strains, yea, just catches the whispering first notes: she strains to hear the last trump. For the trumpet shall sound, at the last, I say, the trumpet shall sound, and the dead, all those who died in the Lord, all the living in Christ who shall be changed, the dead shall be raised incorruptible.

For this corruptible must put on incorruption; and this mortal must put on immortality. So when this corruptible shall have put on incorruption, and this mortal shall have put on immortality, then shall be brought to pass the saying that is written, Death is swallowed up in victory. And so shall we ever be with the Lord. That is, all the elect; namely, every one of the faith of God's elect. Saving faith.

This is the faith, the saving faith, that has been faithfully set forth and described in the preceding pages of this book, as the Lord shall bear witness in the last day, according to the word of the everlasting God, according to the testimony of the Spirit. Now therefore, take heed, the more earnest heed, take heed to these things, for they are the things, the infallible things, that accompany salvation. 'He that hath an ear, let him hear what the Spirit saith unto the churches.'

'I Jesus have sent mine angel to testify unto you these things in the churches.' 'He which testifieth these things saith, Surely I come quickly.' Even so, come, Lord Jesus. The grace of our Lord Jesus Christ be with you all. Amen.

JOHN METCALFE

INDEX

TO OTHER PUBLICATIONS

PSALMS, HYMNS AND SPIRITUAL SONGS

THE PSALMS

OF THE

OLD TESTAMENT

The Psalms of the Old Testament, the result of years of painstaking labour, is an original translation into verse from the Authorised Version, which seeks to present the Psalms in the purest scriptural form possible for singing. Here, for the first time, divine names are rendered as and when they occur in the scripture, the distinction between LORD and Lord has been preserved, and every essential point of doctrine and experience appears with unique perception and fidelity.

The Psalms of the Old Testament is the first part of a trilogy written by John Metcalfe, the second part of which is entitled *Spiritual Songs from the Gospels*, and the last, *The Hymns of the New Testament*. These titles provide unique and accurate metrical versions of passages from the psalms, the gospels and the new testament epistles respectively, and are intended to be used together in the worship of God.

Price £2.50 *(postage extra)*
(hard-case binding, dust-jacket)
ISBN 0 9506366 7 3

SPIRITUAL SONGS

FROM

THE GOSPELS

The *Spiritual Songs from the Gospels*, the result of years of painstaking labour, is an original translation into verse from the Authorised Version, which seeks to present essential parts of the gospels in the purest scriptural form possible for singing. The careful selection from Matthew, Mark, Luke and John, set forth in metrical verse of the highest integrity, enables the singer to sing 'the word of Christ' as if from the scripture itself, 'richly and in all wisdom'; and, above all, in a way that facilitates worship in song of unprecedented fidelity.

The *Spiritual Songs from the Gospels* is the central part of a trilogy written by John Metcalfe, the first part of which is entitled *The Psalms of the Old Testament*, and the last, *The Hymns of the New Testament*. These titles provide unique and accurate metrical versions of passages from the psalms, the gospels and the new testament epistles respectively, and are intended to be used together in the worship of God.

Price £2.50 *(postage extra)*
(hard-case binding, dust-jacket)
ISBN 0 9506366 8 1

THE HYMNS

OF THE

NEW TESTAMENT

The *Hymns of the New Testament*, the result of years of painstaking labour, is an original translation into verse from the Authorised Version, which presents essential parts of the new testament epistles in the purest scriptural form possible for singing. The careful selection from the book of Acts to that of Revelation, set forth in metrical verse of the highest integrity, enables the singer to sing 'the word of Christ' as if from the scripture itself, 'richly and in all wisdom'; and, above all, in a way that facilitates worship in song of unprecedented fidelity.

The *Hymns of the New Testament* is the last part of a trilogy written by John Metcalfe, the first part of which is entitled *The Psalms of the Old Testament*, and the next, *Spiritual Songs from the Gospels*. These titles provide unique and accurate metrical versions of passages from the psalms, the gospels and the new testament epistles respectively, and are intended to be used together in the worship of God.

Price £2.50 *(postage extra)*
(hard-case binding, dust-jacket)
ISBN 0 9506366 9 X

'THE APOSTOLIC FOUNDATION OF THE CHRISTIAN CHURCH' SERIES

FOUNDATIONS UNCOVERED

THE APOSTOLIC FOUNDATION
OF THE
CHRISTIAN CHURCH

Volume I

Foundations Uncovered is a small book of some 37 pages. This is the introduction to the major series: 'The Apostolic Foundation of the Christian Church'.

Rich in truth, the Introduction deals comprehensively with the foundation of the apostolic faith under the descriptive titles: The Word, The Doctrine, The Truth, The Gospel, The Faith, The New Testament, and The Foundation.

The contents of the book reveal: The Fact of the Foundation; The Foundation Uncovered; What the Foundation is not; How the Foundation is Described; and, Being Built upon the Foundation.

'This book comes with the freshness of a new Reformation.'

Price 30p *(postage extra)*
(Laminated cover)
ISBN 0 9506366 5 7

THE BIRTH OF JESUS CHRIST

THE APOSTOLIC FOUNDATION
OF THE
CHRISTIAN CHURCH

Volume II

'The very spirit of adoration and worship rings through the pages of *The Birth of Jesus Christ*.

'The author expresses with great clarity the truths revealed to him in his study of holy scriptures at depth. We are presented here with a totally lofty view of the Incarnation.

'John Metcalfe is to be classed amongst the foremost expositors of our age; and his writings have about them that quality of timelessness that makes me sure they will one day take their place among the heritage of truly great Christian works.'

From a review by Rev. David Catterson.

'Uncompromisingly faithful to scripture ... has much to offer which is worth serious consideration ... deeply moving.'

The Expository Times.

Price 95p *(postage extra)*
(Laminated Cover)
ISBN 0 9502515 5 0

THE MESSIAH

THE APOSTOLIC FOUNDATION
OF THE
CHRISTIAN CHURCH

Volume III

The Messiah is a spiritually penetrating and entirely original exposition of Matthew chapter one to chapter seven from the trenchant pen of John Metcalfe.

Matthew Chapters One to Seven

GENEALOGY · BIRTH · STAR OF BETHLEHEM
HEROD · FLIGHT TO EGYPT · NAZARETH
JOHN THE BAPTIST · THE BAPTIST'S MINISTRY
JESUS' BAPTISM · ALL RIGHTEOUSNESS FULFILLED
HEAVEN OPENED · THE SPIRIT'S DESCENT
THE TEMPTATION OF JESUS IN THE WILDERNESS
JESUS' MANIFESTATION · THE CALLING · THE TRUE DISCIPLES
THE BEATITUDES · THE SERMON ON THE MOUNT

'Something of the fire of the ancient Hebrew prophet ......
Metcalfe has spiritual and expository potentials of a high order.'

The Life of Faith.

Price £2.45 *(postage extra)*
(425 pages, Laminated Cover)
ISBN 0 9502515 8 5

THE SON OF GOD AND SEED OF DAVID

THE APOSTOLIC FOUNDATION
OF THE
CHRISTIAN CHURCH

Volume IV

The Son of God and Seed of David is the fourth volume in
the major work entitled 'The Apostolic Foundation of the
Christian Church.'

'The author proceeds to open and allege that Jesus Christ is
and ever was *The Son of God*. This greatest of subjects, this
most profound of all mysteries, is handled with reverence and
with outstanding perception.

'The second part considers *The Seed of David*. What is meant
precisely by 'the seed'? And why 'of David'? With prophetic
insight the author expounds these essential verities.'

Price £6.95 *(postage extra)*
Hardback 250 pages
Laminated bookjacket
ISBN 1 870039 16 5

CHRIST CRUCIFIED

THE APOSTOLIC FOUNDATION
OF THE
CHRISTIAN CHURCH

Volume V

Christ Crucified the definitive work on the crucifixion, the blood, and the cross of Jesus Christ.

The crucifixion of Jesus Christ witnessed in the Gospels: the gospel according to Matthew; Mark; Luke; John.

The blood of Jesus Christ declared in the Epistles: the shed blood; the blood of purchase; redemption through his blood; the blood of sprinkling; the blood of the covenant.

The doctrine of the cross revealed in the apostolic foundation of the Christian church: the doctrine of the cross; the cross and the body of sin; the cross and the carnal mind; the cross and the law; the offence of the cross; the cross of our Lord Jesus Christ.

Price £6.95 *(postage extra)*
Hardback 300 pages
Laminated bookjacket
ISBN 1 870039 08 4

JUSTIFICATION BY FAITH

THE APOSTOLIC FOUNDATION
OF THE
CHRISTIAN CHURCH

Volume VI

THE HEART OF THE GOSPEL · THE FOUNDATION OF THE CHURCH
THE ISSUE OF ETERNITY
CLEARLY, ORIGINALLY AND POWERFULLY OPENED

The basis · The righteousness of the law
The righteousness of God · The atonement · Justification
Traditional views considered · Righteousness imputed to faith
Faith counted for righteousness · Justification by Faith

*'And it came to pass, when Jesus had ended these sayings, the people
were astonished at his doctrine: for he taught them as one having
authority, and not as the scribes.' Matthew 7:28,29.*

Price £7.50 *(postage extra)*
Hardback 375 pages
Laminated bookjacket
ISBN 1870039 11 4

THE CHURCH: WHAT IS IT?

THE APOSTOLIC FOUNDATION
OF THE
CHRISTIAN CHURCH

Volume VII

The answer to this question proceeds first from the lips of Jesus himself, Mt. 16:18, later to be expounded by the words of the apostles whom he sent.

Neither fear of man nor favour from the world remotely affect the answer.

Here is the truth, the whole truth, and nothing but the truth.

The complete originality, the vast range, and the total fearlessness of this book command the attention in a way that is unique.

Read this book: you will never read another like it.

Outspokenly devastating yet devastatingly constructive.

Price £7.75 (postage extra)
Hardback 400 pages
Laminated bookjacket
ISBN 1 870039 23 8

OTHER TITLES

NOAH AND THE FLOOD

Noah and the Flood expounds with vital urgency the man and the message that heralded the end of the old world. The description of the flood itself is vividly realistic. The whole work has an unmistakable ring of authority, and speaks as 'Thus saith the Lord'.

'Mr. Metcalfe makes a skilful use of persuasive eloquence as he challenges the reality of one's profession of faith ... he gives a rousing call to a searching self-examination and evaluation of one's spiritual experience.'

The Monthly Record of the Free Church of Scotland.

Price £1.90 *(postage extra)*
(Laminated Cover)
ISBN 1 870039 22 X

DIVINE FOOTSTEPS

Divine Footsteps traces the pathway of the feet of the Son of man from the very beginning in the prophetic figures of the true in the old testament through the reality in the new; doing so in a way of experimental spirituality. At the last a glimpse of the coming glory is beheld as his feet are viewed as standing at the latter day upon the earth.

Price 95p *(postage extra)*
(Laminated Cover)
ISBN 1 870039 21 1

THE RED HEIFER

The Red Heifer was the name given to a sacrifice used by the children of Israel in the Old Testament—as recorded in Numbers 19—in which a heifer was slain and burned. Cedar wood, hyssop and scarlet were cast into the burning, and the ashes were mingled with running water and put in a vessel. It was kept for the children of Israel for a water of separation: it was a purification for sin.

In this unusual book the sacrifice is brought up to date and its relevance to the church today is shown.

Price 75p *(postage extra)*
ISBN 0 9502515 4 2

THE WELLS OF SALVATION

The Wells of Salvation is written from a series of seven powerful addresses preached at Tylers Green. It is a forthright and experimental exposition of Isaiah 12:3, 'Therefore with joy shall ye draw water out of the wells of salvation.'

Price £1.50 *(postage extra)*
(Laminated Cover)
ISBN 0 9502515 6 9

OF GOD OR MAN?

LIGHT FROM GALATIANS

The Epistle to the Galatians contends for deliverance from the law and from carnal ministry.

The Apostle opens his matter in two ways:

Firstly, Paul vindicates himself and his ministry against those that came not from God above, but from Jerusalem below.

Secondly, he defends the Gospel and evangelical liberty against legal perversions and bondage to the flesh.

Price £1.45 *(postage extra)*
(Laminated Cover)
ISBN 0 9506366 3 0

A QUESTION FOR POPE JOHN PAUL II

As a consequence of his many years spent apart in prayer, lonely vigil, and painstaking study of the scripture, John Metcalfe asks a question and looks for an answer from Pope John Paul II.

Price £1.25. *(postage extra)*
(Laminated Cover)
ISBN 0 9506366 4 9

THE BOOK OF RUTH

The Book of Ruth is set against the farming background of old testament Israel at the time of the Judges, the narrative—unfolding the work of God in redemption—being marked by a series of agricultural events.

These events—the famine; the barley harvest; the wheat harvest; the winnowing—possessed a hidden spiritual significance to that community, but, much more, they speak in figure directly to our own times, as the book reveals.

Equally contemporary appear the characters of Ruth, Naomi, Boaz, and the first kinsman, drawn with spiritual perception greatly to the profit of the reader.

Price £4.95 *(postage extra)*
Hardback 200 pages
Laminated bookjacket
ISBN 1 870039 17 3

PRESENT-DAY CONVERSIONS
OF THE NEW TESTAMENT KIND

FROM THE MINISTRY OF

JOHN METCALFE

The outstandingly striking presentation of this fascinating paperback will surely catch the eye, as its title and contents will certainly captivate the mind: here is a unique publication.

Woven into a gripping narrative, over twenty-one short life stories, all centred on conversions that simply could not have happened had not God broken in, and had not Christ been revealed, the book presents a tremendous challenge, at once moving and thrilling to the reader.

Price £2.25 (*postage extra*)
(Laminated Cover)
ISBN 1 870039 31 9

DIVINE MEDITATIONS

OF

WILLIAM HUNTINGTON

Originally published by Mr. Huntington as a series of letters to J. Jenkins, under the title of 'Contemplations on the God of Israel', the spiritual content of this correspondence has been skilfully and sympathetically edited, abridged, and arranged so as to form a series of meditations, suitable for daily readings.

Mr. Huntington's own text is thereby adapted to speak directly to the reader in a way much more suited to his ministering immediately to ourselves, in our own circumstances and times.

It is greatly hoped that many today will benefit from this adaption which carefully retains both the spirit and the letter of the text. If any prefer the original format, this is readily available from several sources and many libraries.

Nevertheless, the publishers believe the much more readable form into which Mr. Huntington's very words have been adapted will appeal to a far wider audience, for whose comfort and consolation this carefully edited work has been published.

Price £2.35 *(postage extra)*
(Laminated Cover)
ISBN 1 870039 24 6

'TRACT FOR THE TIMES' SERIES

THE GOSPEL OF GOD

'TRACT FOR THE TIMES' SERIES

The Gospel of God. Beautifully designed, this tract positively describes the gospel under the following headings: The Gospel is of God; The Gospel is Entirely of God; The Gospel is Entire in Itself; The Gospel is Preached; The Gospel Imparts Christ; and, Nothing But the Gospel Imparts Christ.

Price 25p *(postage extra)*
(Laminated Cover)
No. 1 in the Series

THE STRAIT GATE

'TRACT FOR THE TIMES' SERIES

The Strait Gate. Exceptionally well made, this booklet consists of extracts from 'The Messiah', compiled in such a way as to challenge the shallowness of much of today's 'easy-believism', whilst positively pointing to the strait gate.

Price 25p *(postage extra)*
(Laminated Cover)
No. 2 in the Series

ETERNAL SONSHIP
AND TAYLOR BRETHREN

'TRACT FOR THE TIMES' SERIES

Eternal Sonship and Taylor Brethren. This booklet is highly recommended, particularly for those perplexed by James Taylor's teaching against the eternal sonship of Christ.

Price 25p *(postage extra)*
(Laminated Cover)
No. 3 in the Series

MARKS OF THE
NEW TESTAMENT CHURCH
'TRACT FOR THE TIMES' SERIES

Marks of the New Testament Church. This exposition from Acts 2:42 declares what were, and what were not, the abiding marks of the church. The apostles' doctrine, fellowship and ordinances are lucidly explained.

Price 25p *(postage extra)*
(Laminated Cover)
No. 4 in the Series

THE CHARISMATIC DELUSION
'TRACT FOR THE TIMES' SERIES

The Charismatic Delusion. A prophetic message revealing the fundamental error of this movement which has swept away so many in the tide of its popularity. Here the delusion is dispelled.

Price 25p *(postage extra)*
(Laminated Cover)
No. 5 in the Series

PREMILLENNIALISM EXPOSED
'TRACT FOR THE TIMES' SERIES

Premillennialism Exposed. Well received evangelically, particularly through the influence of J.N. Darby, the Schofield bible, and the Plymouth Brethren, Premillennialism has assumed the cloak of orthodoxy. In this tract the cloak is removed, and the unorthodoxy of this system is exposed. A remarkable revelation.

Price 25p *(postage extra)*
(Laminated Cover)
No. 6 in the Series

JUSTIFICATION AND PEACE

'TRACT FOR THE TIMES' SERIES

Justification and Peace. This tract is taken from a message preached in December 1984 at Penang Hill, Malaysia. In this well-known address, peace with God is seen to be based upon nothing save justification by faith. No one should miss this tract.

Price 25p *(postage extra)*
(Laminated Cover)
No. 7 in the Series

FAITH OR PRESUMPTION?

'TRACT FOR THE TIMES' SERIES

Faith or presumption? The eighth tract in this vital series exposes the difference between faith and presumption, showing that faith is not of the law, neither is is apart from the work of God, nor is it of man. The work of God in man that precedes saving faith is opened generally and particularly, and the tract goes on to reveal positively the nature of saving faith. Belief and 'easy-believism' are contrasted, making clear the difference between the two, as the system of presumption—called easy-believism—is clearly shown, and the way of true belief pointed out with lucid clarity.

Price 25p *(postage extra)*
(Laminated Cover)
No. 8 in the Series

THE ELECT UNDECEIVED

'TRACT FOR THE TIMES' SERIES

The Elect undeceived, the ninth Tract for the Times, earnestly contends for 'the faith once delivered to the saints' in a way that is spiritually edifying, positive, and subject to the Lord Jesus Christ according to the scriptures.

The Tract is a response to the pamphlet 'Salvation and the Church' published jointly by the Catholic Truth Society and Church House Publishing, in which the Anglican and Roman Catholic Commissioners agree together about JUSTIFICATION. The pamphlet shows how they have agreed.

Price 25p *(postage extra)*
(Laminated Cover)
No. 9 in the Series

JUSTIFYING RIGHTEOUSNESS

'TRACT FOR THE TIMES' SERIES

Justifying Righteousness. Was it wrought by the law of Moses or by the blood of Christ? Written not in the language of dead theology but that of the living God, here is the vital and experimental doctrine of the new testament. Part of the book 'Justification by Faith', nevertheless this tract has a message in itself essential to those who would know and understand the truth.

Price 25p *(postage extra)*
(Laminated Cover)
No. 10 in the Series

RIGHTEOUSNESS IMPUTED
'TRACT FOR THE TIMES' SERIES

Righteousness Imputed. The truth of the gospel and the fallacy of tradition. Here the gospel trumpet of the jubilee is sounded in no uncertain terms, as on the one hand that truth essential to be believed for salvation is opened from holy scripture, and on the other the errors of Brethrenism are brought to light in a unique and enlightening way. This tract is taken from the book 'Justification by Faith', but in itself it conveys a message of great penetration and clarity.

Price 25p *(postage extra)*
(Laminated Cover)
No. 11 in the Series

THE GREAT DECEPTION
'TRACT FOR THE TIMES' SERIES

The Great Deception. The erosion of Justification by faith. All ministers, every Christian, and each assembly ought not only to possess but to read and reread this prophetic message as the word of the Lord to this generation, set in the context of the age. This tract is part of the book 'Justification by Faith' but contains within itself a message which is at once vital and authoritative.

Price 25p *(postage extra)*
(Laminated Cover)
No. 12 in the Series

A FAMINE IN THE LAND

'TRACT FOR THE TIMES' SERIES

A Famine in the Land. Taken from the Book of Ruth, with telling forcefulness this tract opens conditions exactly parallel to those of our own times. 'Behold, the days come, saith the Lord GOD, that I will send a famine in the land, not a famine of bread, nor a thirst for water, but of hearing the words of the LORD: and they shall wander from sea to sea, and from the north even to the east, they shall run to and fro to seek the word of the LORD, and shall not find it.'

Price 25p *(postage extra)*
(Laminated Cover)
No. 13 in the Series

BLOOD AND WATER

'TRACT FOR THE TIMES' SERIES

Blood and Water. Of the four gospels, only John reveals the truth that blood was shed at the cross. When it was shed, Jesus was dead already. With the blood there came forth water. But what do these things mean? With devastating present-day application, this tract tells you what they mean.

Price 25p *(postage extra)*
(Laminated Cover)
No. 14 in the Series

WOMEN BISHOPS?
'TRACT FOR THE TIMES' SERIES

Women Bishops? This is a question that has arisen in America, but should it have arisen at all?
Read this tract and find out the authoritative answer.

Price 25p *(postage extra)*
(Laminated Cover)
No. 15 in the Series

THE HEAVENLY VISION
'TRACT FOR THE TIMES' SERIES

The Heavenly Vision not only transformed the prophet himself, it became a savour of life unto life—or death unto death—to all the people.
'Where there is no vision the people perish', Proverbs 29:18. This is true. But where is the vision today? And what is the vision today? This tract answers those questions.

Price 25p *(Postage extra)*
(Laminated Cover)
No. 16 in the Series

EVANGELICAL TRACTS

EVANGELICAL TRACTS

1. **The Two Prayers of Elijah.** Green card cover, price 10p.

2. **Wounded for our Transgressions.** Gold card cover, price 10p.

3. **The Blood of Sprinkling.** Red card cover, price 10p.

4. **The Grace of God that brings Salvation.** Blue card cover, price 10p.

5. **The Name of Jesus.** Rose card cover, price 10p.

6. **The Ministry of the New Testament.** Purple card cover, price 10p.

7. **The Death of the Righteous** (*The closing days of J.B. Stoney*) by A.M.S. (his daughter). Ivory card cover, Price 10p.

8. **Repentance.** Sky blue card cover, price 10p.

9. **Legal Deceivers Exposed.** Crimson card cover, price 10p.

ECCLESIA TRACTS

ECCLESIA TRACTS

The Beginning of the Ecclesia by John Metcalfe. No. 1 in the Series, Sand grain cover, Price 10p.

Churches and the Church by J.N. Darby. Edited. No. 2 in the Series, Sand grain cover, Price 10p.

The Ministers of Christ by John Metcalfe. No. 3 in the Series, Sand grain cover, Price 10p.

The Inward Witness by George Fox. Edited. No. 4 in the Series, Sand grain cover, Price 10p.

The Notion of a Clergyman by J.N. Darby. Edited. No. 5 in the Series, Sand grain cover, Price 10p.

The Servant of the Lord by William Huntington. Edited and Abridged. No. 6 in the Series, Sand grain cover, Price 10p.

One Spirit by William Kelly. Edited. No. 7 in the Series, Sand grain cover, Price 10p.

The Funeral of Arminianism by William Huntington. Edited and Abridged. No. 8 in the Series, Sand grain cover, Price 10p.

One Body by William Kelly. Edited. No. 9 in the Series, Sand grain cover, Price 10p.

False Churches and True by John Metcalfe. No. 10 in the Series, Sand grain cover, Price 10p.

Separation from Evil by J.N. Darby. Edited. No. 11 in the Series, Sand grain cover, Price 10p.

The Remnant by J.B. Stoney. Edited. No. 12 in the Series, Sand grain cover, Price 10p.

MINISTRY BY JOHN METCALFE

TAPE MINISTRY BY JOHN METCALFE
FROM ENGLAND AND THE FAR EAST
IS AVAILABLE.

In order to obtain this free recorded ministry, please send your blank cassette (C.90) and the cost of the return postage, including your name and address in block capitals, to the John Metcalfe Publishing Trust, Church Road, Tylers Green, Penn, Bucks, HP10 8LN. Tapelists are available on request.

Owing to the increased demand for the tape ministry, we are unable to supply more than two tapes per order, except in the case of meetings for the hearing of tapes, where a special arrangement can be made.

THE MINISTRY OF THE NEW TESTAMENT

The purpose of this substantial A4 gloss paper magazine is to provide spiritual and experimental ministry with sound doctrine which rightly and prophetically divides the Word of Truth.

Readers of our books will already know the high standards of our publications. They can be confident that these pages will maintain that quality, by giving access to enduring ministry from the past, much of which is derived from sources that are virtually unobtainable today, and publishing a living ministry from the present. Selected articles from the following writers have already been included:

ELI ASHDOWN · ABRAHAM BOOTH · JOHN BUNYAN
JOHN BURGON · JOHN CALVIN · DONALD CARGILL
JOHN CENNICK · J.N. DARBY · GEORGE FOX · JOHN FOXE
WILLIAM GADSBY · WILLIAM HUNTINGTON · WILLIAM KELLY
JOHN KENNEDY · JOHN KERSHAW · HANSERD KNOLLYS
JAMES LEWIS · MARTIN LUTHER · ROBERT MURRAY McCHEYNE
JOHN METCALFE · ALEXANDER—SANDY—PEDEN · J.C. PHILPOT
J.K. POPHAM · JAMES RENWICK · J.B. STONEY · HENRY TANNER
ARTHUR TRIGGS · JOHN VINALL · JOHN WARBURTON
JOHN WELWOOD · GEORGE WHITEFIELD · J.A. WYLIE

Price £1.75 (*postage included*)
Issued Spring, Summer, Autumn, Winter.

Book Order Form

Please send to the address below:-

	Price	Quantity
A Question for Pope John Paul II	£1.25	......
Of God or Man?	£1.45	......
Noah and the Flood	£1.90	......
Divine Footsteps	£0.95	......
The Red Heifer	£0.75	......
The Wells of Salvation	£1.50	......
The Book of Ruth (Hardback edition)	£4.95	......
Divine Meditations of William Huntington	£2.35	......
Present-Day Conversions of the New Testament Kind	£2.25	......
Saving Faith	£2.25	......
Deliverance from the Law	£1.90	......

Psalms, Hymns & Spiritual Songs (Hardback edition)

	Price	Quantity
The Psalms of the Old Testament	£2.50	......
Spiritual Songs from the Gospels	£2.50	......
The Hymns of the New Testament	£2.50	......

'Apostolic Foundation of the Christian Church' series

		Price	Quantity
Foundations Uncovered	Vol.I	£0.30	......
The Birth of Jesus Christ	Vol.II	£0.95	......
The Messiah	Vol.III	£2.45	......
The Son of God and Seed of David (Hardback edition)	Vol.IV	£6.95	......
Christ Crucified (Hardback edition)	Vol.V	£6.95	......
Justification by Faith (Hardback edition)	Vol.VI	£7.50	......
The Church: What is it? (Hardback edition)	Vol.VII	£7.75	......

Name and Address (in block capitals)

. . . .

. . . .

. . . .

If money is sent with order please allow for postage. Please address to:- The
John Metcalfe Publishing Trust, Church Road, Tylers Green, Penn, Bucks, HP10 8LN.

Tract Order Form

Please send to the address below:-

		Price	Quantity
Evangelical Tracts			
The Two Prayers of Elijah		£0.10	......
Wounded for our Transgressions		£0.10	......
The Blood of Sprinkling		£0.10	......
The Grace of God that Brings Salvation		£0.10	......
The Name of Jesus		£0.10	......
The Ministry of the New Testament		£0.10	......
The Death of the Righteous by A.M.S.		£0.10	......
Repentance		£0.10	......
Legal Deceivers Exposed		£0.10	......
'Tract for the Times' series			
The Gospel of God	No.1	£0.25	......
The Strait Gate	No.2	£0.25	......
Eternal Sonship and Taylor Brethren	No.3	£0.25	......
Marks of the New Testament Church	No.4	£0.25	......
The Charismatic Delusion	No.5	£0.25	......
Premillennialism Exposed	No.6	£0.25	......
Justification and Peace	No.7	£0.25	......
Faith or presumption?	No.8	£0.25	......
The Elect undeceived	No.9	£0.25	......
Justifying Righteousness	No.10	£0.25	......
Righteousness Imputed	No.11	£0.25	......
The Great Deception	No.12	£0.25	......
A Famine in the Land	No.13	£0.25	......
Blood and Water	No.14	£0.25	......
Women Bishops?	No.15	£0.25	......
The Heavenly Vision	No.16	£0.25	......
Ecclesia Tracts			
The Beginning of the Ecclesia	No.1	£0.10	......
Churches and the Church (J.N.D.)	No.2	£0.10	......
The Ministers of Christ	No.3	£0.10	......
The Inward Witness (G.F.)	No.4	£0.10	......
The Notion of a Clergyman (J.N.D.)	No.5	£0.10	......
The Servant of the Lord (W.H.)	No.6	£0.10	......
One Spirit (W.K.)	No.7	£0.10	......
The Funeral of Arminianism (W.H.)	No.8	£0.10	......
One Body (W.K.)	No.9	£0.10	......
False Churches and True	No.10	£0.10	......
Separation from Evil (J.N.D.)	No.11	£0.10	......
The Remnant (J.B.S.)	No.12	£0.10	......

Name and Address (in block capitals)

. . . .

. . . .

. . . .

If money is sent with order please allow for postage. Please address to:- The
John Metcalfe Publishing Trust, Church Road, Tylers Green, Penn, Bucks, HP10 8LN.

Magazine Order Form

Name and Address (in block capitals)

....
....
....

Please send me .... current copy/copies of The Ministry of the New Testament.

Please send me .... year/s subscription.

  I enclose a cheque/postal order for £ ....

(Price: including postage, U.K. £1.75; Overseas £1.90)
(One year's subscription: Including postage, U.K. £7.00; Overseas £7.60)

Cheques should be made payable to The John Metcalfe Publishing Trust, and for overseas subscribers should be in pounds sterling drawn on a London Bank.

10 or more copies to one address will qualify for a 10% discount

Back numbers from Spring 1986 available.

Please send to The John Metcalfe Publishing Trust, Church Road, Tylers Green, Penn, Bucks, HP10 8LN

All Publications of the Trust are subsidised by the Publishers.